Carol Hopkins

Civil War Legacies III

A Treasury of Quilts for Reproduction-Fabric Lovers

Martingale®
Create with Confidence

Dedication

To my husband, Edward; my children, Tim, Emily, and Mike; my children's loves, Sara, Kris, and Carly; and my children's little ones, Allie, Alik, Maret, and Mallie. You all fill my life with incredible joy and happiness.

Civil War Legacies III:
A Treasury of Quilts for Reproduction-Fabric Lovers

That Patchwork Place® An Imprint of Martingale

Martingale® Create with Confidence

Martingale®
19021 120th Ave. NE, Ste. 102
Bothell, WA 98011-9511 USA
ShopMartingale.com

Printed in China
21 20 19 18 17 16 8 7 6 5 4 3 2 1

Library of Congress Cataloging-in-Publication Data
is available upon request.

ISBN: 978-1-60468-748-4

MISSION STATEMENT

We empower makers who use fabric and yarn to make life more enjoyable.

CREDITS

PUBLISHER AND
CHIEF VISIONARY OFFICER
Jennifer Erbe Keltner

CONTENT DIRECTOR
Karen Costello Soltys

MANAGING EDITOR
Tina Cook

ACQUISITIONS EDITOR
Karen M. Burns

TECHNICAL EDITOR
Monique Dillard

COPY EDITOR
Sheila Chapman Ryan

DESIGN MANAGER
Adrienne Smitke

COVER AND
INTERIOR DESIGNER
Regina Girard

PHOTOGRAPHER
Brent Kane

ILLUSTRATOR
Anne Moscicki

Contents

Introduction

I offer my heartfelt thanks to those of you who purchased *Civil War Legacies* and *Civil War Legacies II,* and then asked for more patterns to showcase quilt blocks and fabrics reproduced from the Civil War era. I'm happy to present this new collection of 16 small quilts that are a range of doll quilts, baby quilts, table toppers, and wall hangings.

Anywhere you display these quilts, their warm colors will blend with almost any color scheme—and add eye-catching pops of color to the neutral palette found in many of our homes. I display mine by draping them inside of baskets, rolling them up and standing them on end in old pottery and crocks, stacking them in a tall glass bookcase, covering antique doll beds, and arranging them in small groupings on walls as though they were pictures.

In fact, I decorate with so many of these little quilts that my youngest son once asked if we were moving when he came home from school one afternoon and wondered why the family room looked bare, unaware that I was preparing for a quilt-guild presentation. My granddaughter thinks they are perfect coverings for her American Girl doll, and my nieces used to wrap them around their skinny little bodies as though they were spa towels.

No matter where or how you use them, all of the machine-pieced scrap quilts in *Civil War Legacies III* are easy to make and don't require a long attention span, a major commitment of time, or yards of fabric to end up with a small treasure. With the assortment of precuts available in quilt shops, a charm pack, Layer Cake, or fat-quarter bundle may be all you need to make the small blocks in many of these quilts. Or, challenge your quilting friends to make a chosen pattern, and organize a "small pieces" fabric swap to get things started. And finally, there's always your stash to draw from, or as a sign I purchased recently called it, your "extensive private textile collection," that you've been saving for just the right quilt.

You're holding 16 patterns in your hand right now, all of them whispering "pick me, pick me!" It's time to get busy creating your own legacy.

Skedaddler

In addition to paying monetary fines, Civil War soldiers found guilty of inappropriate behavior often received other unusual punishments following their military court-martial. Private William Thompson, found guilty of desertion, was paraded before his regiment two hours a day for five days wearing a sign with the word "Skedaddler" written on it.

Materials

Yardage is based on 42"-wide fabric.

1¼ yards of directional tan print *OR* ⅝ yard of nondirectional tan print for outer border

½ yard of brown stripe for setting squares

½ yard of light print for blocks

¼ yard of red print for inner border

36 assorted dark scraps, at least 3" x 5", for blocks

18 assorted medium scraps, at least 3" x 5", for blocks

⅓ yard of brown print for binding

1⅜ yards of fabric for backing

38" x 46" piece of batting

To Add Interest

When arranging the finished blocks prior to sewing your quilt top together, rotate some blocks so that the medium and dark fabrics in the four-patch units are in different positions.

Cutting

All measurements include ¼"-wide seam allowances.

From the light print, cut:

6 strips, 1⅞" x 42"; crosscut into 108 squares, 1⅞" x 1⅞". Cut each square in half diagonally to yield 216 triangles.

From *18* of the dark scraps, cut:

2 squares, 1⅞" x 1⅞" (36 total)

From *each* of the remaining 18 dark scraps, cut:

2 squares, 1⅞" x 1⅞"; cut in half diagonally to yield 4 triangles (72 total)

From *each* of the medium scraps, cut:

2 squares, 1⅞" x 1⅞" (36 total)

From the brown stripe, cut:

2 strips, 4½" x 42"; crosscut into 17 squares, 4½" x 4½"

From the red print, cut:

4 strips, 1¼" x 42"

From the *lengthwise grain* of the directional tan print, cut:*

4 strips, 4½" x 42"

From the brown print, cut:

4 strips, 2" x 42"

**If you're using a nondirectional print, cut the strips across the fabric width.*

"Skedaddler," pieced by Carol Hopkins and quilted by Lisa Ramsey

Finished quilt size: 30" x 38"

Finished block size: 4" x 4"

Making the Blocks

For each block, select two matching medium squares, two matching dark squares, and four matching dark triangles. Instructions are for making one block.

1. Sew two matching medium 1⅞" squares and two matching dark 1⅞" squares together to make a four-patch unit measuring 3¼" square. Press the seam allowances open.

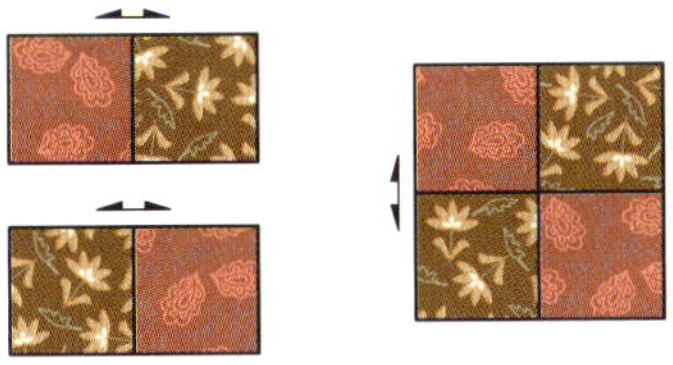

Make 1.

2. Sew a dark triangle to a light triangle to make a half-square-triangle unit. Press the seam allowances toward the dark triangle. Make four matching units measuring 1½" square.

Make 4.

3. Sew two light triangles to each of the half-square-triangles from step 2. Press the seam allowances open. Trim off the dog-ear points.

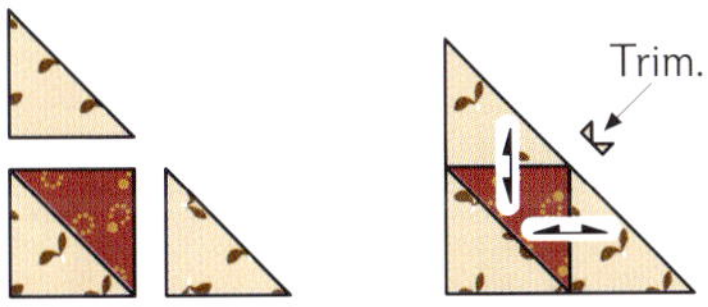

Make 4.

4. Sew two units from step 3 to opposite sides of the four-patch unit. Press the seam allowances open. Sew the remaining two units from step 3 to the four-patch unit and press the seam allowances open to make a block measuring 4½" square. Make 18 blocks.

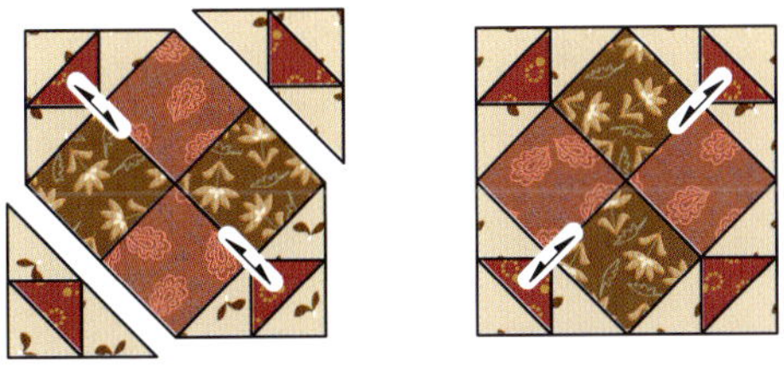

Make 18.

Assembling and Finishing the Quilt

For more help with any of the finishing steps, go to ShopMartingale.com/HowtoQuilt.

1. Arrange the blocks and brown-stripe squares as shown below. Sew the pieces together in rows and press the seam allowances open.
2. Sew the rows together, pressing the seam allowances open after adding each row.

Quilt assembly

3. For the inner border, measure the length of the quilt top through the center and trim two of the red strips to this measurement. Sew the strips to the sides of the quilt and press the seam allowances toward the border.
4. Measure the width of the quilt through the center, including the just-added border pieces, and trim the two remaining red strips to this measurement. Sew the strips to the top and bottom of the quilt and press the seam allowances toward the border.
5. For the outer border, measure the length of the quilt top through the center and add 10". Trim two tan directional-print strips to this measurement. Pin the strips to the sides of the quilt, right sides

together and matching the centers. Sew these strips to the quilt, starting and stopping ¼" from the corners of the quilt.

6. Measure the quilt width, without the border, and add 10". Trim the two remaining tan strips to this measurement. Center and pin these strips to the top and bottom of the quilt, right sides together. Sew these strips to the quilt, starting and stopping ¼" from the corners of the quilt, and press the seam allowances toward the border.
7. Miter the border at each corner of the quilt.
8. Layer the quilt top, batting, and backing. Baste the layers together and hand or machine quilt as desired. Trim the excess batting and backing fabric.
9. Use the brown strips to bind the quilt. Add a hanging sleeve, if desired, and a label.

Optional Butted-Corner Border

If you'd prefer a butted border to a mitered border, follow these steps for the tan outer borders.

1. Measure the length of the quilt top through the center and trim two of the tan strips to this measurement. Sew the strips to the sides of the quilt and press the seam allowances toward the outer border.
2. Measure the width of the quilt top through the center, including the just-added border pieces, and trim the two remaining tan strips to this measurement. Sew the strips to the top and bottom of the quilt and press the seam allowances toward the outer border.

Adding borders

Home Front

Women and children left behind on the home front experienced many hardships, especially those who were tasked with maintaining small farms while their husbands and fathers went off to fight in the Civil War. Anxious to escape this challenging life, many young boys left home to join the military, only to find it an even harsher life than they'd had at home.

Materials

Yardage is based on 42"-wide fabric.

⅔ yard of turquoise stripe for outer border

⅝ yard of blue small-scale print for setting triangles

½ yard of blue large-scale print for center square and cornerstones

⅓ yard of red large-scale print for inner border

⅓ yard *each* of 4 assorted light prints for blocks

4 assorted brown or black scraps, at least 9" x 9" each, for blocks

4 assorted red scraps, at least 7" x 13" each, for star points

4 assorted medium scraps (2 blue, 1 pink, 1 tan), at least 7" x 7" each, for blocks

8 assorted medium scraps (4 blue, 2 tan, 1 pink, 1 cheddar), at least 5" x 5" each, for small stars

⅜ yard of blue-and-red print for binding

3⅛ yards of fabric for backing

55" x 55" piece of batting

Cutting

All measurements include ¼"-wide seam allowances.

From *each* of the light prints, cut:

1 square, 5¼" x 5¼"; cut into quarters diagonally to yield 4 triangles (16 total)

4 squares, 3½" x 3½" (16 total)

16 squares, 1⅞" x 1⅞"; cut in half diagonally to yield 32 triangles (128 total)

4 squares, 1½" x 1½" (16 total)

From *each* of the brown or black scraps, cut:

4 squares 1½" x 1½" (16 total)

12 squares, 1⅞" x 1⅞"; cut in half diagonally to yield 24 triangles (96 total)

From *each* of the red scraps, cut:

2 squares, 5¼" x 5¼"; cut into quarters diagonally to yield 8 triangles (32 total)

From *each* of the medium 7" x 7" scraps, cut:

1 square, 5¼" x 5¼"; cut into quarters diagonally to yield 4 triangles (16 total)

From *each* of the medium 5" x 5" scraps, cut:

4 squares, 1⅞" x 1⅞"; cut in half diagonally to yield 8 triangles (64 total)

From the blue small-scale print, cut:

1 square, 18¼" x 18¼"; cut into quarters diagonally to yield 4 triangles

2 squares, 9⅜" x 9⅜"; cut in half diagonally to yield 4 triangles

From the blue large-scale print, cut:

1 square, 12½" x 12½"

4 squares, 5" x 5"

From the red large-scale print, cut:

4 strips, 2" x 42"

From the turquoise stripe, cut:

4 strips, 5" x 42"

From the blue-and-red print, cut:

5 strips, 2" x 42"

"Home Front," pieced by Carol Hopkins and quilted by Lisa Ramsey

Finished quilt size: 46½" x 46½"

Finished block size: 12" x 12"

Making the Feathered Star Blocks

Instructions are for making one block.

1. Sew a light 1⅞" triangle to a black or brown 1⅞" triangle to make a half-square-triangle unit. Press the seam allowances toward the black or brown triangle. Make 24 matching units measuring 1½" square.

Make 24.

2. Sew together three half-square-triangle units as shown. Press the seam allowances open. Make four.

Make 4.

3. Sew together three half-square-triangle units and a matching black or brown 1½" square as shown. Press the seam allowances open. Make four.

Make 4.

4. Arrange the units from steps 2 and 3 and a light 3½" square as shown. Sew the pieces into rows and press the seam allowances open. Sew the rows together, pressing the seam allowances open, to make a unit measuring 4½" square. Make four.

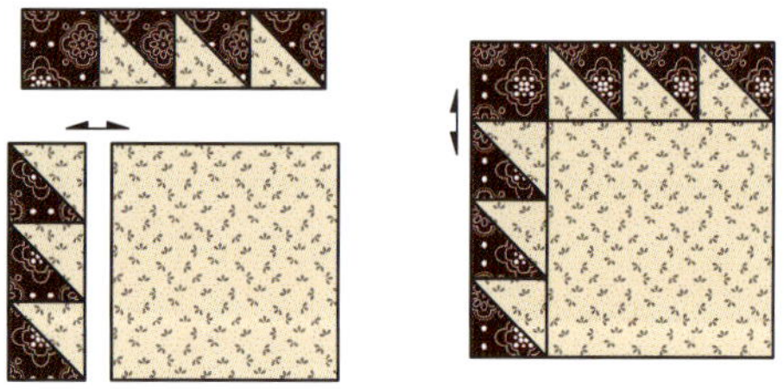

Make 4.

5. Sew together two matching red 5¼" triangles, one light 5¼" triangle, and one pink, tan, or blue 5¼" triangle to make a quarter-square-triangle measuring 4½" square. Make four.

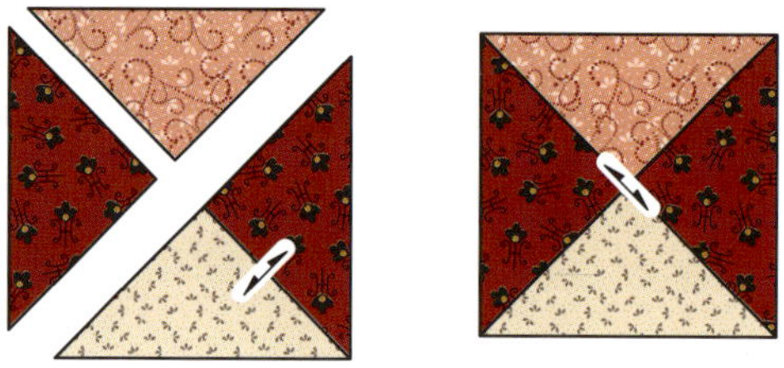

Make 4.

6. Using the 1⅞" triangles, sew together four light/four blue triangles, four light/four medium triangles, and four blue/four medium triangles to make a total of 12 half-square-triangles. Press the seam allowances toward the darker triangles.

Make 4. Make 4. Make 4.

7. Arrange the half-square-triangle units from step 6 and four light 1½" squares as shown. Sew the pieces together into rows and press the seam allowances open. Then sew the rows together, pressing the seam allowances open to make a star unit measuring 4½" square.

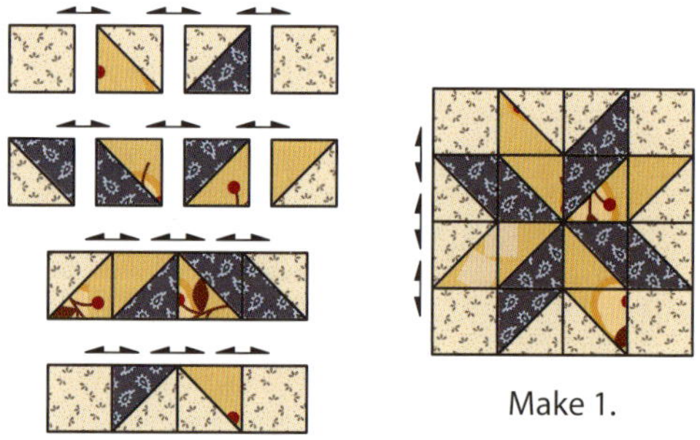

Make 1.

8. Arrange the units from steps 4, 5, and 7 as shown. Sew the units together into rows and press the seam allowances open. Sew the rows together, pressing the seam allowances open to

make a block measuring 12½" square. Make four Feathered Star blocks.

Make 4.

Assembling and Finishing the Quilt

For more help with any of the finishing steps, go to ShopMartingale.com/HowtoQuilt.

1. Arrange the Feathered Star blocks and the blue large-scale center square in diagonal rows as shown below. Add the blue small-scale 18¼" side triangles and 9⅜" corner triangles.
2. Sew the blocks and side triangles together in diagonal rows. Press the seam allowances open. Add the corner triangles and press the seam allowances toward the triangles.

Quilt asembly

3. Trim the quilt top if necessary, making sure to leave ¼" beyond the points of the blocks for seam allowance.
4. For the inner border, measure the length of the quilt top through the center and trim two red strips to this measurement. Sew the strips to the sides of the quilt and press the seam allowances toward the border.
5. Measure the width of the quilt top through the center, including the just-added border pieces, and trim the two remaining red strips to this measurement. Sew the strips to the top and bottom of the quilt and press the seam allowances toward the border.
6. For the outer border, measure the length of the quilt top through the center and trim four turquoise strips to this measurement. Sew two of the strips to the sides of the quilt and press the seam allowances toward the outer border.
7. Sew blue large-scale 5" squares to both ends of the remaining two turquoise strips. Press the seam allowances open. Sew these strips to the top and bottom of the quilt and press the seam allowances toward the border.

Adding borders

8. Layer the quilt top, batting, and backing. Baste the layers together and hand or machine quilt as desired. Trim the excess batting and backing fabric.
9. Use the blue-and-red strips to bind the quilt. Add a hanging sleeve, if desired, and a label.

Milton's Musket Balls

Civil War soldiers had to make enough musket balls to fill their leather pouches before going into each battle. The soldiers used the campfire to melt lead in an iron kettle. Then, long-handled ladles were used to pour the hot liquid into a mold to form the metal balls. During the battle, the soldiers used gunpowder and rag patches to load and shoot the balls, one at a time, from their muskets.

Materials

Yardage is based on 42"-wide fabric.

⅞ yard of purple-and-brown stripe *OR* ½ yard of nondirectional print for border

⅝ yard of brown print for sashing and binding

⅛ yard of blue print for cornerstones

12 assorted light scraps, at least 6" x 8" each, for blocks

12 assorted dark scraps, at least 8" x 8" each, for blocks

1⅛ yards of fabric for backing

34" x 40" piece of batting

To Add Interest

Select sashing and cornerstone fabrics that are close to the colors in the striped border to create a blended, low-contrast look for your quilt. If you want the blocks to pop, select a sashing fabric with strong color contrast.

Cutting

All measurements include ¼"-wide seam allowances.

From *each* of the assorted light scraps, cut:

2 squares, 1⅞" x 1⅞"; cut in half diagonally to yield 4 triangles (48 total)

9 squares, 1½" x 1½" (108 total)

From *each* of the assorted dark scraps, cut:

2 squares, 1⅞" x 1⅞"; cut in half diagonally to yield 4 triangles (48 total)

12 squares, 1½" x 1½" (144 total)

From the brown print, cut:

5 strips, 1½" x 42"; crosscut into 31 rectangles, 1½" x 5½"

4 strips, 2" x 42"

From the blue print, cut:

1 strip, 1½" x 42"; crosscut into 20 squares, 1½" x 1½"

From the *lengthwise grain* of the purple-and-brown stripe, cut:*

4 strips, 3½" x 28"

**If you're using a nondirectional print, cut the strips across the fabric width.*

Making the Blocks

Each block contains one light and one dark print. Instructions are for making one block.

1. Sew a dark triangle to a light triangle to make a half-square-triangle unit. Press the seam allowances toward the dark triangle. Make four matching units measuring 1½" square.

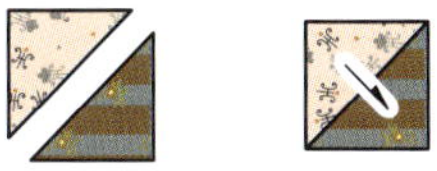

Make 4.

"Milton's Musket Balls," pieced by Carol Hopkins and quilted by Lisa Ramsey

Finished quilt size: 25½" x 31½"

Finished block size: 5" x 5"

2. Arrange the half-square-triangle units from step 1, nine matching light 1½" squares, and 12 matching dark 1½" squares as shown. Sew the pieces together into rows and press the seam allowances open. Sew the rows together, pressing the seam allowances open to make a block measuring 5½" square. Make 12 blocks.

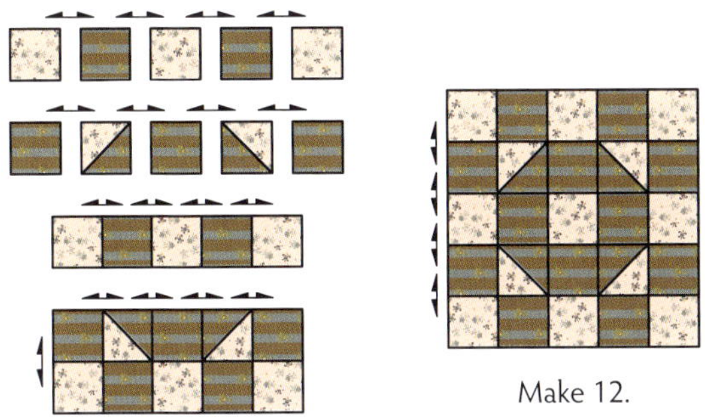
Make 12.

Assembling and Finishing the Quilt

For more help with any of the finishing steps, go to ShopMartingale.com/HowtoQuilt.

1. Arrange the blocks, brown sashing rectangles, and blue cornerstones as shown. Sew the pieces together in rows and press the seam allowances open. Sew the rows together, pressing the seam allowances open after adding each row.

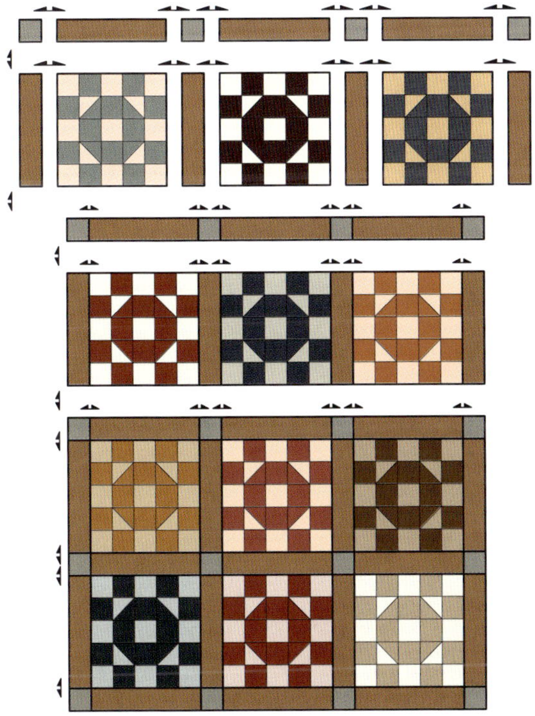
Quilt assembly

2. Measure the length of the quilt through the center and trim two of the purple-and-brown strips to this measurement. Sew the strips to the sides of the quilt and press the seam allowances toward the border.
3. Measure the width of the quilt top through the center, including the just-added border pieces, and trim the two remaining purple-and-brown strips to this measurement. Sew the strips to the top and bottom of the quilt and press the seam allowances toward the border.

Adding borders

4. Layer the quilt top, batting, and backing. Baste the layers together and hand or machine quilt as desired. Trim the excess batting and backing fabric.
5. Use the brown strips to bind the quilt. Add a hanging sleeve, if desired, and a label.

Poppy Ladies

The red flowers on this quilt remind me of the time my mother and I collected donations for paper poppies on Veteran's Day while standing on the front steps of a Pittsburgh bank. I remember feeling like such an important six-year-old as people dropped money into the slot of the can I was holding.

Materials

Yardage is based on 42"-wide fabric.

1⅓ yards of red plaid for outer border

¾ yard of cheddar print for setting squares and triangles

12 assorted light prints, at least 9" x 14" each, for blocks and pieced border

12 assorted red prints, at least 9" x 14" each, for blocks and pieced border

⅜ yard of cheddar stripe for binding

3 yards of fabric for backing

46" x 54" piece of batting

To Add Interest

Don't match your red fabrics too closely. Instead, select a mix of bright reds, brownish reds, madder reds, and reds prints containing other colors.

Cutting

All measurements include ¼-wide seam allowances.

From *each* of the light prints, cut:

1 square, 3⅞" x 3⅞"; cut in half diagonally to yield 2 triangles (24 total)

2 squares, 3¼" x 3¼" (24 total)

11 squares, 1⅞" x 1⅞"; cut in half diagonally to yield 22 triangles (264 total; 12 are extra)

From *each* of the red prints, cut:

1 square, 3½" x 3½" (12 total)

1 square, 2⅞" x 2⅞"; cut in half diagonally to yield 2 triangles (24 total)

1 square, 2¾" x 2¾" (12 total)

1 square, 2½" x 2½" (12 total)

10 squares, 1⅞" x 1⅞"; cut in half diagonally to yield 20 triangles (240 total; 12 are extra)

From the cheddar print, cut:

1 strip, 9¾" x 42"; crosscut into 3 squares, 9¾" x 9¾". Cut each square into quarters diagonally to yield 12 triangles (2 are extra).

1 strip, 6½" x 42"; crosscut into 6 squares, 6½" x 6½"

1 strip, 5⅛" x 42"; crosscut into 2 squares, 5⅛" x 5⅛". Cut each square in half diagonally to yield 4 triangles

From the *lengthwise grain* of the red plaid, cut:

4 strips, 5¼" x 42"

From the cheddar stripe, cut:

4 strips, 2" x 42"

Making the Blocks

Each block contains one red and one light print. Instructions are for making one block.

1. Sew a red 1⅞" triangle to a light 1⅞" triangle to make a half-square-triangle unit. Press the seam allowances toward the red triangle. Make nine matching units measuring 1½" square.

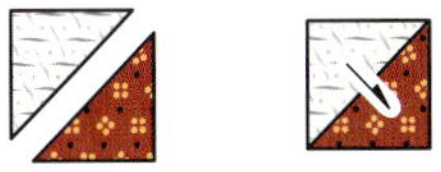

Make 9.

"Poppy Ladies," pieced by Carol Hopkins and quilted by Carol Alberts

Finished quilt size: 37½" x 46"

Finished block size: 6" x 6"

2. Sew two half-square-triangle units together as shown. Press the seam allowances open. Sew this unit to a red 2½" square and press the seam allowances open.

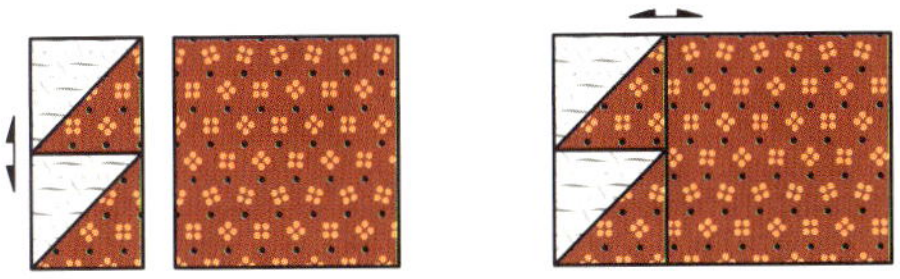

3. Sew three half-square-triangle units together as shown. Press the seam allowances open. Sew this unit to the unit from step 2 and press the seam allowances open.

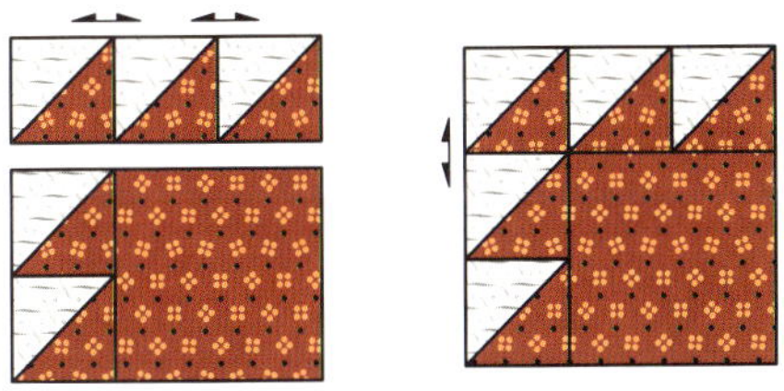

4. Sew a light 1⅞" triangle to two half-square-triangle units as shown. Press the seam allowances open. Sew this unit to a red 2⅞" triangle and press the seam allowances open.

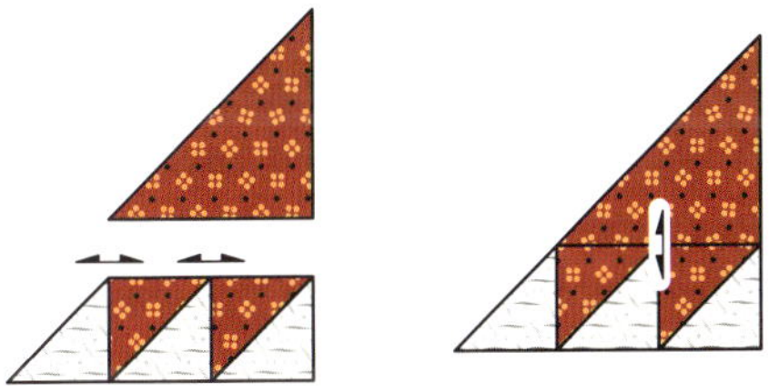

5. Sew the unit from step 4 to a light 3⅞" triangle and press the seam allowances open.

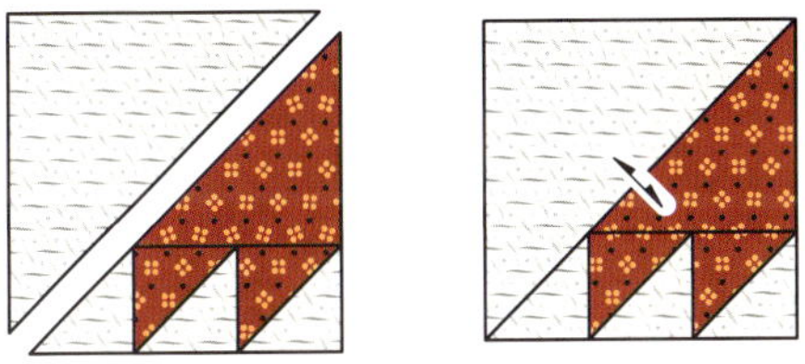

6. Sew a light 1⅞" triangle to two half-square triangles as shown. Press the seam allowances open. Sew this unit to a 2⅞" red triangle and press the seam allowances open.

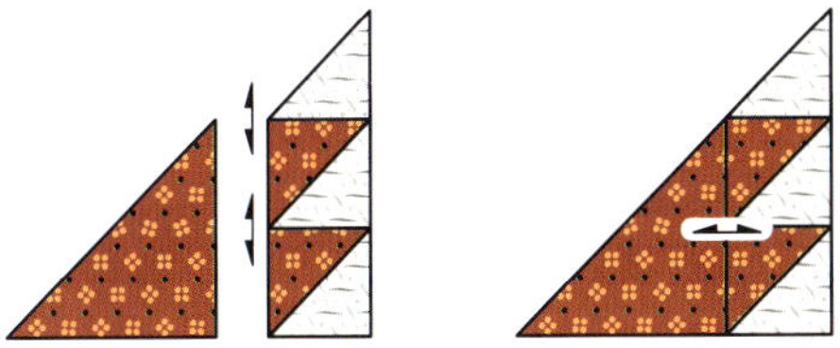

7. Sew the unit from step 6 to a light 3⅞" triangle and press the seam allowances open.

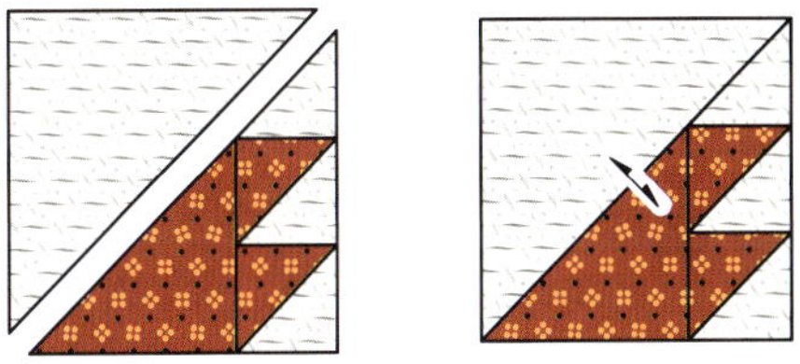

8. Place a light 3¼" square on a red 3½" square, right sides together. Sew diagonally from corner to corner of the light square, fold it back toward the corner, and press. Trim out the middle layer of fabric, leaving a ¼" seam allowance. Repeat on the opposite corner of the same red square using another light 3¼" square.

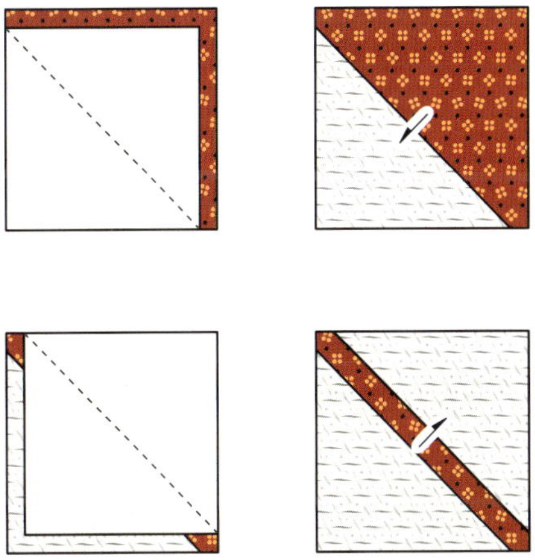

Ellie's Tea Garden

When Uncle Eddie introduced us to Ellie, his wife-to-be, I thought she had a wonderful last name *and* she was what I wanted to be when I grew up—an elementary school teacher. The former Miss Teegarden always made special things for her family and friends, and then to top it off, she became a quilter! So even though I've taken liberties with the spelling of her name, the pinks in this garden are for my Aunt Ellie. I imagine her as a gentle Southern lady, had she lived during the Civil War era.

Materials

Yardage is based on 42"-wide fabric.

⅜ yard of pink-and-brown print for outer border and binding

⅛ yard of pink stripe for inner border

18 assorted pink scraps, at least 3" x 3" each, for blocks

18 assorted brown scraps, at least 3" x 3" each, for blocks

17 assorted light scraps, at least 3" x 3" each, for setting squares

¾ yard of fabric for backing

22" x 25" piece of batting

To Add Interest

Fabrics with stripes, checks, and dots add character to this little quilt.

Cutting

All measurements include ¼"-wide seam allowances.

From *each* of the brown scraps, cut:
4 squares, 1¼" x 1¼" (72 total)

From *each* of the pink scraps, cut:
1 square, 2" x 2" (18 total)

From *each* of the light scraps, cut:
1 square, 2" x 2" (17 total)

From the pink stripe, cut:
2 strips, 1" x 42"; cut in half crosswise to yield 4 strips

From the pink-and-brown print, cut:
2 strips, 3" x 42"; cut in half crosswise to yield 4 strips
2 strips, 2" x 42"

Making the Square-in-a-Square Blocks

Each block contains a different pink and brown fabric. Instructions are for making one block.

Sew matching brown 1¼" squares to each corner of a pink 2" square to make a Square-in-a Square block. Press as shown after adding each square. Make 18 blocks.

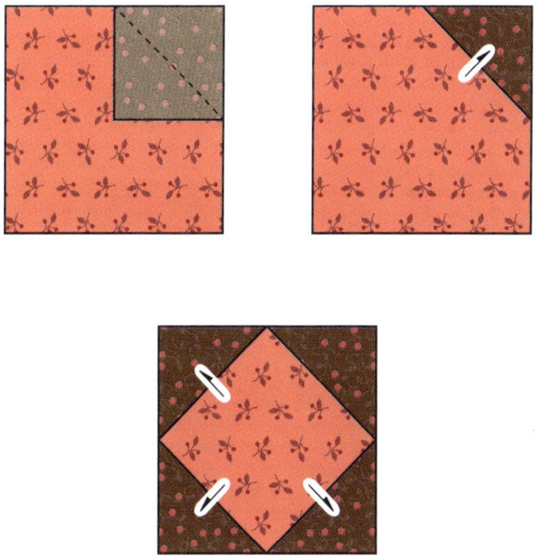

Make 18.

"Ellie's Tea Garden," pieced and quilted by Carol Hopkins

Finished quilt size: 14" x 17"

Finished block size: 1½" x 1½"

Assembling and Finishing the Quilt

For more help with any of the finishing steps, go to ShopMartingale.com/HowtoQuilt.

1. Arrange the blocks and setting squares as shown. Sew the blocks and setting squares together in rows and press the seam allowances open. Sew the rows together, pressing the seam allowances open after adding each row.

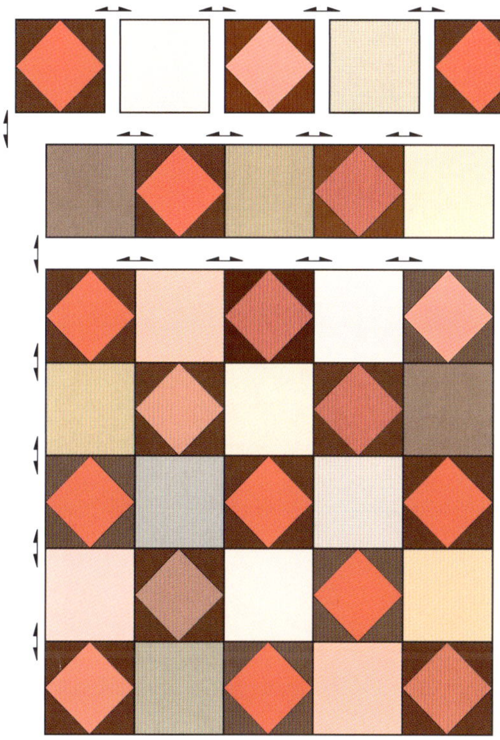

Quilt assembly

2. For the inner border, measure the length of the quilt top through the center and trim two of the pink-stripe strips to this measurement. Sew the strips to the sides of the quilt and press the seam allowances toward the border.

3. Measure the width of the quilt through the center, including the just-added border pieces, and trim the two remaining pink-stripe strips to this measurement. Sew the strips to the top and bottom of the quilt and press the seam allowances toward the border.

4. For the outer border, repeat steps 2 and 3 using the pink-and-brown 3"-wide strips.

Adding borders

5. Layer the quilt top, batting, and backing. Baste the layers together and hand or machine quilt as desired. Trim the excess batting and backing fabric.

6. Use the pink-and-brown 2"-wide strips to bind the quilt. Add a hanging sleeve, if desired, and a label.

Honeysuckle

I think of lush southern gardens when I hear the word honeysuckle. Fortunately, its growing zone is not restricted to the south. When I sit on my back porch in Indiana, I'm treated to the sweet scent of the honeysuckle that climbs over my neighbor's backyard fence. The colors of the delicate flowers on the twisted vines growing over the gray boards inspired the name of this quilt.

Materials

Yardage is based on 42"-wide fabric.

1⅓ yards of large-scale red print for border

1⅓ yards of brown print for setting strips

¾ yard of taupe print for setting triangles

24 assorted light scraps, at least 7" x 7" each, for blocks

24 assorted medium scraps, at least 5" x 5" each, for blocks

24 assorted dark scraps, at least 4" x 7" each, for blocks

⅓ yard of dark-red print for binding

3⅓ yards of fabric for backing

51" x 59" piece of batting

To Add Interest

To create a soft, worn-and-loved look, select fabrics for the setting triangles and setting strips that have a low contrast with the block backgrounds.

Cutting

All measurements include ¼"-wide seam allowances.

From *each* of the light scraps, cut:

4 rectangles, 1¾" x 3" (96 total)

2 squares, 2⅛" x 2⅛"; cut in half diagonally to yield four triangles (96 total)

From *each* of the medium scraps, cut:

4 squares, 1¾" x 1¾" (96 total)

From *each* of the dark scraps, cut:

2 squares, 2⅛" x 2⅛"; cut in half diagonally to yield four triangles (96 total)

From the taupe print, cut:

2 strips, 8⅜" x 42"; crosscut into 10 squares, 8⅜" x 8⅜". Cut each square into quarters diagonally to yield 40 triangles.

1 strip, 4½" x 42"; crosscut into 8 squares, 4½" x 4½". Cut each square in half diagonally to yield 16 triangles.

From the *lengthwise grain* of the brown print, cut:

3 strips, 2½" x 47"

From the *lengthwise grain* of the large-scale red print, cut:

4 strips, 4¼" x 47"

From the dark-red print, cut:

5 strips, 2" x 42"

Fabric Saver

If you prefer, the long setting strips can be pieced, requiring less fabric yardage. You'll need ⅓ yard.

"Honeysuckle," pieced by Carol Hopkins and quilted by Lisa Ramsey

Finished quilt size: 42¼" x 50½"

Finished block size: 5" x 5"

Making the Blocks

Each block consists of one light, one medium, and one dark print. Instructions are for making one block.

1. Sew a dark triangle to a light triangle to make a half-square-triangle unit. Press the seam allowances toward the dark triangle. Make four matching units measuring 1¾" square.

Make 4.

2. Sew a medium 1¾" square to the left side of each half-square-triangle unit from step 1 and press the seam allowances open. Make four.

Make 4.

3. Sew a light 1¾" x 3" rectangle to the bottom of each unit from step 2 and press the seam allowances open. Make four.

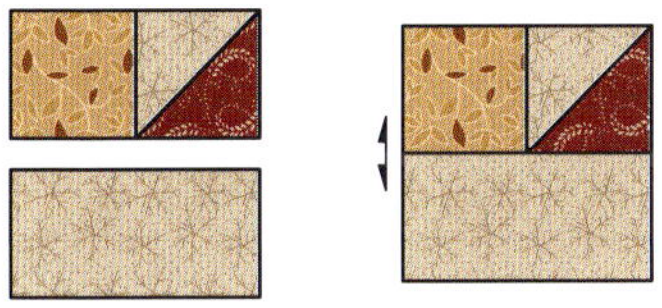

Make 4.

4. Arrange the units from step 3 as shown. Sew the units together in rows, pressing the seam allowances open. Sew the rows together and press the seam allowances open to complete a block measuring 5½" square. Make 24 blocks.

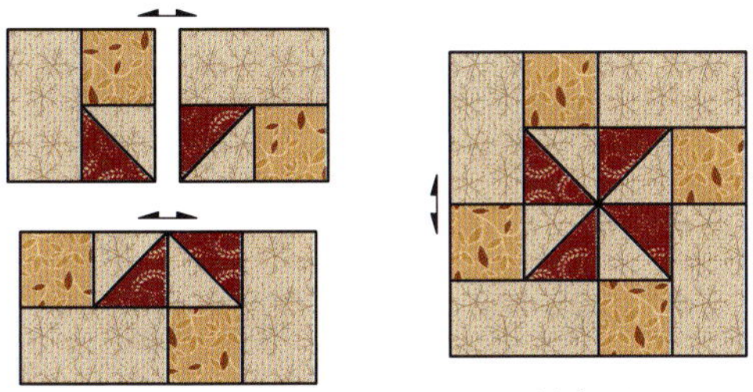

Make 24.

Assembling and Finishing the Quilt

For more help with any of the finishing steps, go to ShopMartingale.com/HowtoQuilt.

1. Sew six blocks and 10 taupe 8⅜" triangles together as shown below to make a row. Press the seam allowances open. Make four rows.
2. Add taupe 4½" triangles to the corners of each row. Press the seam allowances toward the triangles. Trim the rows if necessary, making sure to leave ¼" beyond the points of the blocks for seam allowance.

Make 4.

3. Measure the length of the rows in step 2 and trim the three brown strips to this measurement.

4. Arrange the block rows and brown setting strips as shown. Sew the strips together, pressing the seam allowances open after adding each strip.

Quilt assembly

5. Measure the length of the quilt top through the center and trim two of the large-scale red strips to this measurement. Sew the strips to the sides of the quilt and press the seam allowances toward the border.

6. Measure the width of the quilt top through the center, including the just-added border pieces, and trim the two remaining red strips to this measurement. Sew the strips to the top and bottom of the quilt and press the seam allowances toward the border.

Adding borders

7. Layer the quilt top, batting, and backing. Baste the layers together and hand or machine quilt as desired. Trim the excess batting and backing fabric.

8. Use the dark-red strips to bind the quilt. Add a hanging sleeve, if desired, and a label.

Grandfather Mountain

Tucking her short hair under a forage cap, Malinda Blalock signed her enlistment papers as S. M. Blalock and left her home in Grandfather Mountain, North Carolina, to secretly serve beside Keith, her Confederate-soldier husband. Keith, however, intended to slip through the lines and join up with a Yankee unit. Through a series of unplanned events, including a bullet wound in Malinda's left shoulder that led to the discovery that she was a woman, the Blalocks found themselves returning home to Grandfather Mountain where Keith became a recruiting officer for a Michigan regiment. One account called the Blalocks the "Bonnie and Clyde of the mountains," feared by Northerners and Southerners alike for their bushwhacking, thieving, and murderous acts during the Civil War.

Materials

Yardage is based on 42"-wide fabric.

1 yard of pink-and-brown stripe *OR* ¼ yard of nondirectional print for inner border

⅔ yard of blue print for outer border and binding

¼ yard of tan print for setting triangles

18 assorted light scraps, at least 5" x 5" each, for blocks

18 assorted brown scraps, at least 5" x 5" each, for blocks

18 assorted pink scraps, at least 3" x 5" each, for blocks

18 assorted blue scraps, at least 6" x 6" each, for blocks

1⅛ yards of fabric for backing

33" x 39" piece of batting

To Add Interest

Look for interesting segments within wide-striped fabrics to use as inner borders on your quilts. Fussy cut selected portions of the stripe so that all the borders are identical, and center the design on all sides of the quilt. Stripes like this often result in a clever corner effect without mitering.

Cutting

All measurements include ¼"-wide seam allowances.

From *each* of the light scraps, cut:

3 squares, 1⅞" x 1⅞"; cut in half to yield 6 triangles (108 total)

From *each* of the brown scraps, cut:

3 squares, 1⅞" x 1⅞"; cut in half diagonally to yield 6 triangles (108 total)

From *each* of the pink scraps, cut:

2 squares, 1⅞" x 1⅞"; cut in half diagonally to yield 4 triangles (72 total)

From *each* of the blue scraps, cut:

1 square, 4⅞" x 4⅞"; cut in half diagonally to yield 2 triangles (36 total; 18 are extra)

From the tan print, cut:

1 strip, 7" x 42"; crosscut into:

- 3 squares, 7" x 7"; cut into quarters diagonally to yield 12 triangles (2 are extra)
- 2 squares, 3¾" x 3¾"; cut in half diagonally to yield 4 triangles

From the *lengthwise grain* of the pink-and-brown stripe, cut*:

4 strips, 1¾" x 36"

From the blue print, cut:

4 strips, 3" x 42"

4 strips, 2" x 42"

**If you're using a nondirectional print, cut the strips across the fabric width.*

"Grandfather Mountain," pieced by Carol Hopkins and quilted by Lisa Ramsey

Finished quilt size: 25" x 30⅝"

Finished block size: 4" x 4"

Making the Blocks

For each block, choose one pink, one brown, one blue, and one light print. Instructions are for making one block.

1. Sew a brown triangle to a light triangle to make a half-square-triangle unit. Press the seam allowances toward the brown triangle. Make six matching units measuring 1½" square.

Make 6.

2. Arrange the half-square-triangle units and four matching pink triangles as shown. Sew the pieces together into rows and press the seam allowances open. Sew the rows together, pressing the seam allowances open.

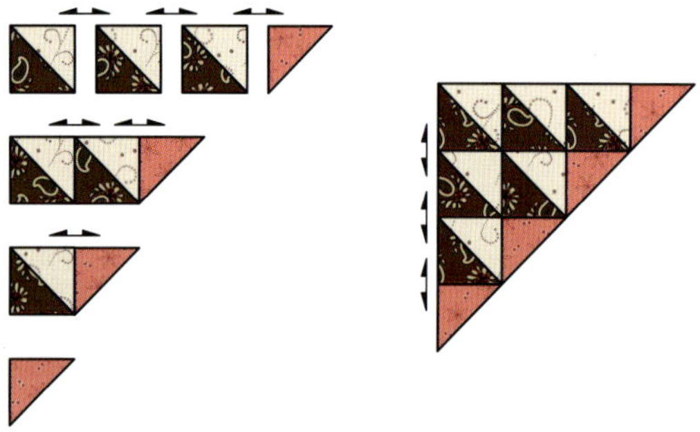

3. Sew the unit from step 2 to a blue triangle and press the seam allowances toward the blue triangle to make a block measuring 4½" square. Make 18 blocks.

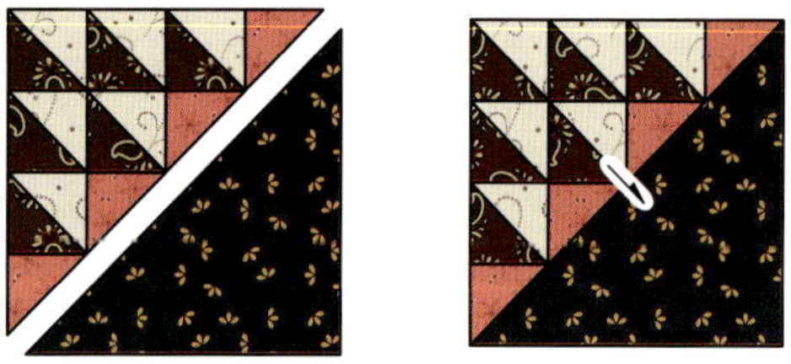

Make 18.

Assembling and Finishing the Quilt

For more help with any of the finishing steps, go to ShopMartingale.com/HowtoQuilt.

1. Arrange the blocks in diagonal rows as shown below. Add the tan 7" side triangles and 3¾" corner triangles.
2. Sew the blocks and side triangles together in diagonal rows. Press the seam allowances open.
3. Sew the rows together, pressing the seam allowances open after adding each row. Add the corner triangles and press the seam allowances toward the triangles.

Quilt assembly

4. Trim the quilt top if necessary, leaving a ¼" seam allowance beyond the points of the blocks.
5. For the inner border, measure the length of the quilt top through the center and add 5". Trim two pink-and-brown strips to this measurement. Pin the strips to the sides of the quilt, right sides together and matching the centers. Sew these strips to the quilt, starting and stopping ¼" from the corners of the quilt.

6. Measure the quilt width, without the border, and add 5". Trim the two remaining pink-and-brown strips to this measurement. Center and pin these strips to the top and bottom of the quilt, starting and stopping ¼" from the corners of the quilt, right sides together. Sew these strips to the quilt and press the seam allowances toward the border, starting and stopping ¼" from the corners of the quilt. Miter the borders at each corner of the quilt.

7. For the outer border, measure the length of the quilt top through the center and trim two of the blue 3"-wide strips to this measurement. Sew the strips to the sides of the quilt and press the seam allowances toward the outer border.

8. Measure the width of the quilt top through the center, including the just-added border pieces, and trim the two remaining blue 3"-wide strips to this measurement. Sew the strips to the top and bottom of the quilt and press the seam allowances toward the outer border.

Adding borders

9. Layer the quilt top, batting, and backing. Baste the layers together and hand or machine quilt as desired. Trim the excess batting and backing fabric.

10. Use the 2"-wide blue strips to bind the quilt. Add a hanging sleeve, if desired, and a label.

Optional Butted-Corner Border

If you've chosen a nondirectional inner-border print, you may prefer not to miter the quilt border. Follow these instructions instead.

1. Measure the length of the quilt top through the center and trim two strips to this measurement. Sew the strips to the sides of the quilt and press the seam allowances toward the border.

2. Measure the width of the quilt top through the center, including the just-added border pieces, and trim the two remaining strips to this measurement. Sew the strips to the top and bottom of the quilt and press the seam allowances toward the border.

Parasol Stars

Parasols of all styles and sizes were an important accessory for Civil War ladies. Usually made from silk fabrics, parasols were intended to provide shade from the harsh southern sun, although some photographs show tiny parasols that seemed to be more fashion-focused than practical. "Carriage parasols" often had short handles that folded up for storage. However, when it rained, these dainty parasols were replaced by large, black umbrellas. It's been reported that the style and use of parasols were often mocked by cartoonists.

Materials

Yardage is based on 42"-wide fabric.

¾ yard of light print for blocks and setting triangles

¾ yard of red print for outer border and binding

¼ yard of turquoise print for inner border

20 assorted medium scraps, at least 7" x 7" each, for blocks

20 assorted dark scraps, at least 7" x 7" each, for blocks

1¼ yards of fabric for backing

40" x 45" piece of batting

To Add Interest

Select a busy, light-colored print with a lot of movement, such as flowers or vines, for the background fabric to prevent seam lines from detracting from the overall design.

Cutting

All measurements include ¼"-wide seam allowances.

From the light print, cut:

1 strip, 7" x 42"; crosscut into:

- 4 squares, 7" x 7"; cut into quarters diagonally to yield 16 triangles (2 are extra)
- 2 squares, 3¾" x 3¾"; cut in half diagonally to yield 4 triangles

10 strips, 1½" x 42"; crosscut into:

- 24 rectangles, 1½" x 4½"
- 104 rectangles, 1½" x 2½"
- 40 squares, 1½" x 1½"

From *each* of the medium scraps, cut:

8 squares, 1½" x 1½" (160 total; 16 are extra)

From *each* of the dark scraps, cut:

10 squares, 1½" x 1½" (200 total; 16 are extra)

From the turquoise print, cut:

4 strips, 1½" x 42"

From the red print, cut:

4 strips, 3½" x 42"

4 strips, 2" x 42"

"Parasol Stars," pieced by Carol Hopkins and quilted by Lisa Ramsey

Finished quilt size: 31⅛" x 36¾"

Finished block size: 4" x 4"

Making the Star Blocks

The light print is paired with a dark and a medium print in each of the blocks. Instructions are for making one block.

1. Make a flying-geese unit with two dark 1½" squares and one light 1½" x 2½" rectangle as shown. Make four matching flying-geese units.

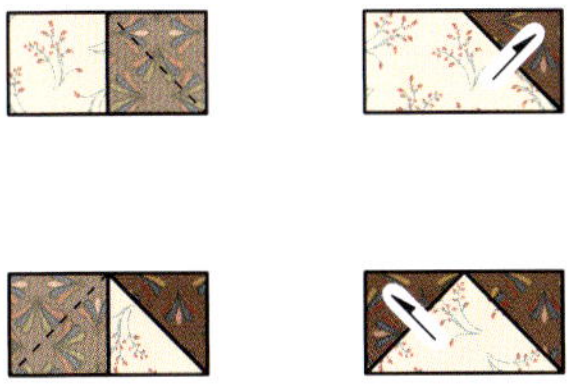

Make 4.

2. Sew two light 1½" squares and two medium 1½" squares together to make a four-patch unit measuring 2½" square. Press the seam allowances open.

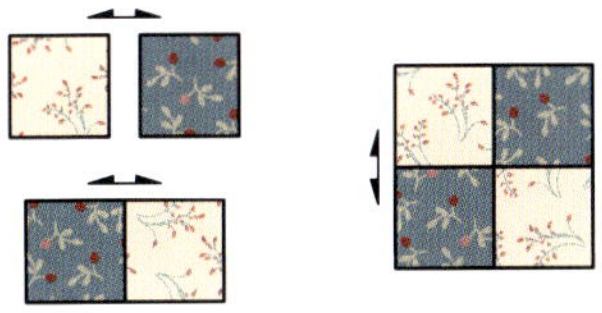

Make 1.

3. Arrange the four flying-geese units, the four-patch unit, and four matching medium 1½" squares as shown. Sew the pieces together in rows and press the seam allowances open. Sew the rows together, pressing seam allowances open to make a block measuring 4½" square. Make 20 Star blocks.

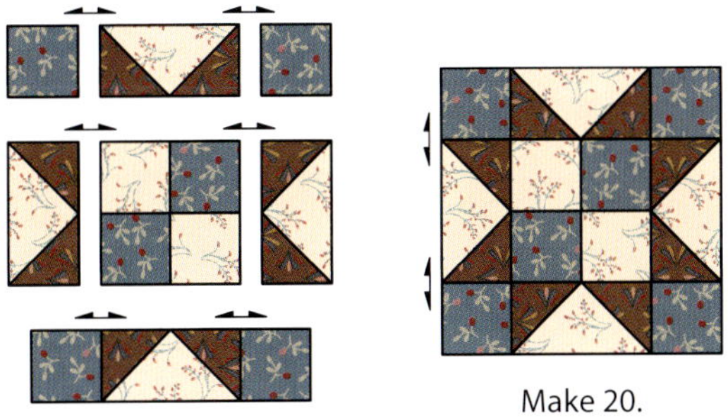

Make 20.

Making the Framed Four Patch Blocks

The light print is paired with a dark and a medium print in each of the blocks. Instructions are for making one block.

1. Sew two medium 1½" squares and two dark 1½" squares together to make a four-patch unit measuring 2½" square. Press the seam allowances open.
2. Sew light 1½" x 2½" rectangles to two sides of the four-patch unit and press the seam allowances open.

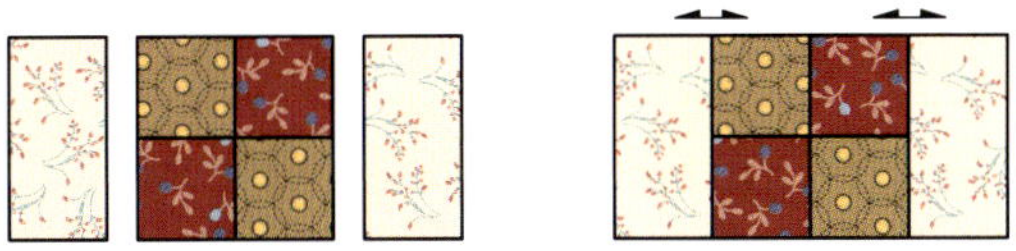

3. Sew two light 1½" x 4½" rectangles to the top and bottom of the unit from step 2 as shown. Press the seam allowances open. Make 12 Framed Four Patch blocks measuring 4½" square.

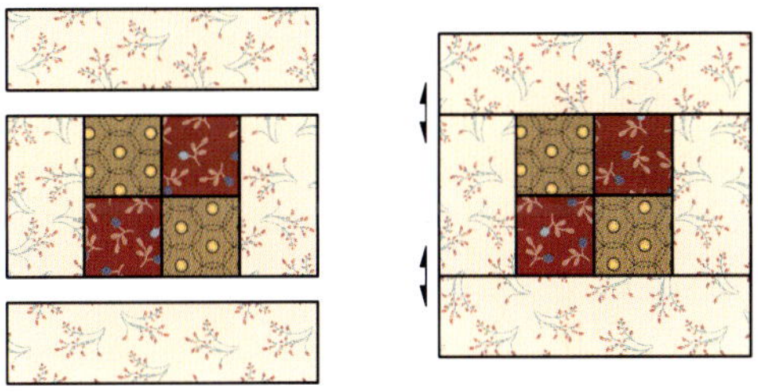

Make 12.

Assembling and Finishing the Quilt

For more help with any of the finishing steps, go to ShopMartingale.com/HowtoQuilt.

1. Arrange the Star blocks and Framed Four Patch blocks in diagonal rows as shown on page 44. Add the light 7" side triangles and 3¾" corner triangles.

2. Sew the blocks and side triangles together in diagonal rows. Press the seam allowances open.
3. Sew the rows together, pressing the seam allowances open after adding each row. Add the corner triangles and press the seam allowances toward the triangles.

Quilt assembly

4. Trim the quilt top if necessary, leaving a ¼" seam allowance beyond the points of the blocks.
5. For the inner border, measure the length of the quilt top through the center and trim two turquoise strips to this measurement. Sew the strips to the sides of the quilt and press the seam allowances toward the border.
6. Measure the width of the quilt top through the center, including the just-added border pieces, and trim the two remaining turquoise strips to this measurement. Sew the strips to the top and bottom of the quilt and press the seam allowances toward the border.
7. Repeat steps 5 and 6 with the red 3½"-wide strips to make the outer border.

Adding borders

8. Layer the quilt top, batting, and backing. Baste the layers together and hand or machine quilt as desired. Trim the excess batting and backing fabric.
9. Use the red 2"-wide strips to bind the quilt. Add a hanging sleeve, if desired, and a label.

Uniform Blues

Faded uniforms, new uniforms, worn uniforms, soiled uniforms—the colors of blue on the battlefield were as varied as the blues in this quilt.

Materials

Yardage is based on 42"-wide fabric.

½ yard of blue stripe for outer border

⅛ yard of navy print for inner border

16 assorted light scraps, at least 10" x 11" each, for blocks and pieced border

16 assorted blue scraps, at least 6" x 9" each, for blocks and pieced border

⅓ yard of dark-blue print for binding

1⅛ yards of fabric for backing

37" x 37" piece of batting

To Add Interest

Select light prints with varying sizes, shapes, and colors of motifs on different shades of white backgrounds.

Cutting

All measurements include ¼"-wide seam allowances.

From *each* of the light scraps, cut:

2 squares, 4⅛" x 4⅛"; cut in half diagonally to yield 4 triangles (64 total; 8 are extra)

1 square, 2⅞" x 2⅞"; cut in half diagonally to yield 2 triangles (32 total)

8 squares, 1½" x 1½" (128 total; 8 are extra)

From *each* of the blue scraps, cut:

1 square, 2⅞" x 2⅞"; cut in half diagonally to yield 2 triangles (32 total)

8 squares, 1½" x 1½" (128 total; 8 are extra)

From the navy print, cut:

2 strips, 1" x 42"; cut in half crosswise to yield 4 strips

From the blue stripe, cut:

4 strips, 3¼" x 42"

From the dark-blue print, cut:

4 strips, 2" x 42"

Making the Blocks

One blue and one light print are used in each block. Instructions are for making one block.

1. Sew a blue 2⅞" triangle to a light 2⅞" triangle to make a half-square-triangle unit. Press the seam allowances toward the blue triangles. Make two matching units measuring 2½" square.

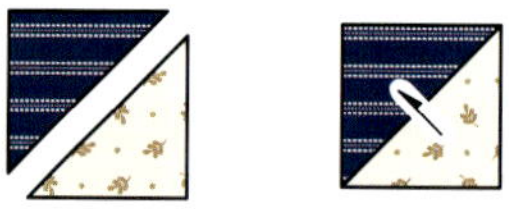

Make 2.

2. Using fabrics matching those in step 1, sew two blue and two light 1½" squares together to make a four-patch unit measuring 2½" square. Press the seam allowances open. Make two.

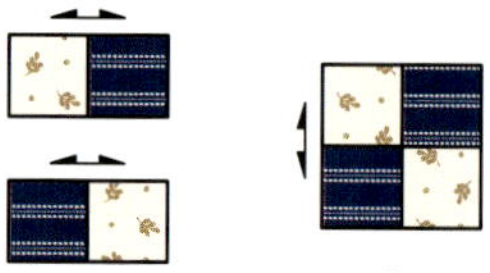

Make 2.

"Uniform Blues," pieced by Carol Hopkins and quilted by Lisa Ramsey

Finished quilt size: 28¾" x 28¾"

Finished block size: 4" x 4"

3. Sew the units into rows as shown, pressing the seam allowances open. Join the rows and press the seam allowances open to make a block measuring 4½" square. Make 16 blocks.

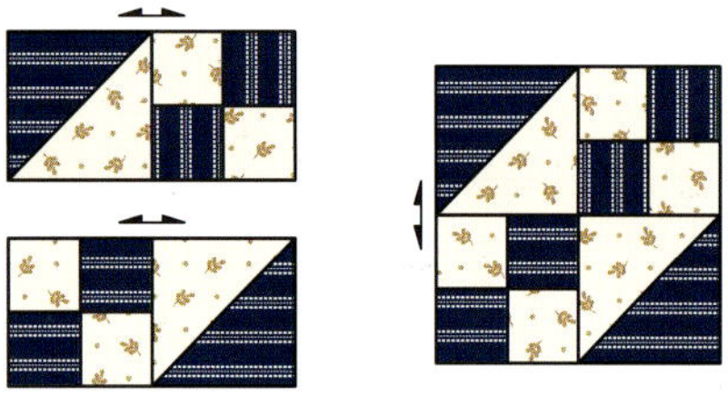

Make 16.

Making the Pieced Border

1. Sew two different blue and two different light 1½" squares together to make a Four Patch block measuring 2½" square. Press the seam allowances open. Make 28 blocks.
2. Arrange seven Four Patch blocks and 14 light 4⅛" triangles as shown. Sew the pieces together in diagonal rows and press the seam allowances open. Sew the rows together, pressing the seam allowances open after adding each row. Trim the excess fabric from the edges as needed, leaving ¼" beyond the points of the blocks for seam allowances. Make four strips.

Make 4.

Assembling and Finishing the Quilt

For more help with any of the finishing steps, go to ShopMartingale.com/HowtoQuilt.

1. Arrange the blocks into rows as shown, paying close attention to the orientation of the four-patch units in each block. Sew the blocks together into rows and press the seam allowances open. Sew the rows together, pressing the seam allowances open after adding each row.

Quilt assembly

2. For the inner border, measure the length of the quilt top through the center and trim two navy 1"-wide strips to this measurement. Sew the strips to the sides of the quilt and press the seam allowances toward the border.
3. Measure the width of the quilt top through the center, including the just-added border pieces, and trim the two remaining navy strips to this measurement. Sew the strips to the top and

bottom of the quilt and press the seam allowances toward the border.

Adding inner borders

4. Sew the short side of a pieced border strip to each side of the quilt, starting and stopping ¼" from the corners of the quilt.

Adding pieced borders

5. Sew the pieced-border strips together where they meet at the corners of the quilt as you would for a mitered corner.

6. For the outer border, repeat steps 2 and 3 using the blue-striped 3¼"-wide strips.

Adding outer borders

7. Layer the quilt top, batting, and backing. Baste the layers together and hand or machine quilt as desired. Trim the excess batting and backing fabric.

8. Use the dark-blue 2"-wide strips to bind the quilt. Add a hanging sleeve, if desired, and a label.

Parlor Music

Parlor music has been called the music of the American Civil War. Gathering to play and listen to music served as a venue for people to share, and live with, the events that dramatically impacted their lives. Religious themes ran throughout the marches and songs. Some say the songs reflected the political ideals of union and states' rights, commemorated heroes and martyrs, celebrated victory, and mourned losses.

Materials

Yardage is based on 42"-wide fabric.

1¼ yards of turquoise print for outer border and binding

20 scraps, at least 6" x 6" each, *OR* ⅞ yard total of assorted light prints for triangles

18 scraps, at least 6" x 6" each, *OR* ⅝ yard total of assorted dark prints for triangles

67 scraps, at least 4" x 4" each, *OR* ½ yard total of assorted light prints for Four Patch blocks

67 scraps, at least 4" x 4" each, *OR* ½ yard total of assorted dark prints for Four Patch blocks

3 yards of fabric for backing

46" x 54" piece of batting

To Add Interest

Use busy, multicolored light and dark prints of various sizes to create visual interest. For more variety, talk a quilting friend into making the quilt at the same time, and then trade units and blocks to acquire a large assortment of fabrics.

Cutting

All measurements include ¼"-wide seam allowances.

From *each* of the 6" x 6" light scraps, cut:

1 square, 5½" x 5½"; cut into quarters diagonally to yield 4 triangles (80 total)

From *each* of the 6" x 6" dark scraps, cut:

1 square, 5½" x 5½"; cut into quarters diagonally to yield 4 triangles (72 total)

From *each* of the 4" x 4" light scraps, cut:

4 squares, 1½" x 1½" (268 total; 2 are extra. Fabrics may be repeated.)

From *each* of the 4" x 4" dark scraps, cut:

4 squares, 1½" x 1½" (268 total; 2 are extra. Fabrics may be repeated.)

From the *lengthwise grain* of the turquoise print, cut:

4 strips, 4" x 45"

4 strips, 2" x 45"

Making the Four Patch Strips

1. Arrange two matching light and two matching dark 1½" squares as shown. Sew the pieces together in rows, and then sew the rows together to make a Four Patch block measuring 2½" square. Press the seam allowances open. Make 133 Four Patch blocks.

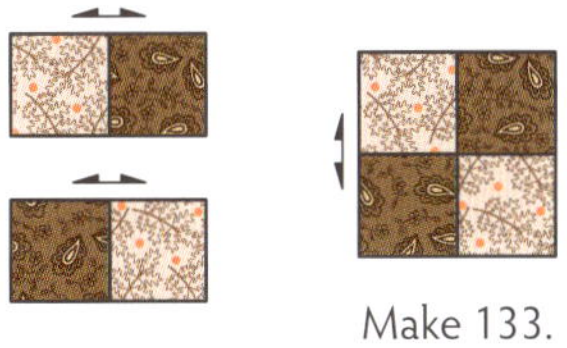

Make 133.

2. Sew 19 Four Patch blocks together to form a strip that measures 2½" x 38½". Press the seam allowances open. Make seven strips of 19 blocks.

Make 7.

"Parlor Music," pieced by Carol Hopkins and quilted by Lisa Ramsey

Finished quilt size: 37½" x 45½"

Finished block size: 2" x 2"

Making the Triangle Strips

1. Beginning with a light 5½" triangle, sew together 10 light triangles and nine dark triangles along the short sides of the triangles, alternating light and dark. The long sides of the triangles should be on the outside edges of the strip. Do not line up the triangles edge to edge; instead, overlap the top triangle over the bottom triangle at a ¼".

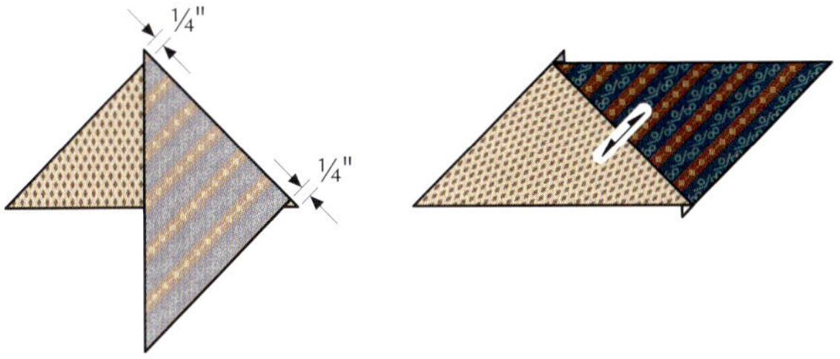

2. Press the seam allowances open after adding each triangle, being careful not to stretch the fabrics. The strip should end with a light triangle. Make eight strips of 19 triangles.

Make 8.

Assembling and Finishing the Quilt

For more help with any of the finishing steps, go to ShopMartingale.com/HowtoQuilt.

1. Beginning with a strip of triangles, arrange alternating strips of Four Patch blocks and triangles.
2. Cut the triangles at the top and bottom of the triangle strips in half crosswise so that they match the length of the Four Patch strips.

Quilt assembly

3. Sew all of the strips together, pressing the seam allowances open after adding each strip.
4. Measure the length of the quilt top through the center and trim two of the turquoise 4"-wide strips to this measurement. Sew the strips to the sides of the quilt and press the seam allowances toward the border.
5. Measure the width of the quilt through the center, including the just-added borders, and trim the two remaining turquoise 4"-wide strips to this measurement. Sew the strips to the top and bottom of the quilt and press the seam allowances toward the border.

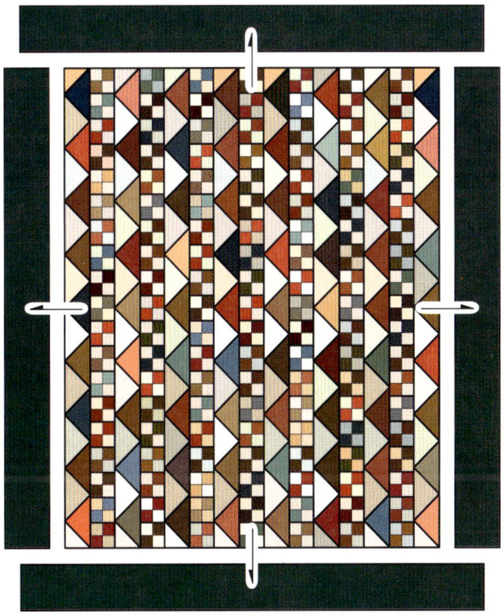

Adding borders

6. Layer the quilt top, batting, and backing. Baste the layers together and hand or machine quilt as desired. Trim the excess batting and backing fabric.
7. Use the turquoise 2"-wide strips to bind the quilt. Add a hanging sleeve, if desired, and a label.

Uncle Frank's Socks

True confession time—I don't really have an Uncle Frank, but I once saw a quilt by that name and decided I'd become his adopted niece so that I, too, could make a quilt in his honor. My imaginary uncle wears argyle socks similar to the blocks in this quilt.

Materials

Yardage is based on 42"-wide fabric.

⅔ yard of green print for outer border and binding

⅛ yard of red print for inner border

12 assorted light scraps, at least 4" x 7" each, for blocks

12 assorted medium scraps, at least 4" x 4" each, for blocks

12 assorted dark scraps, at least 4" x 4" each, for blocks

12 assorted medium or dark scraps, at least 3" x 5" each, for blocks

1 yard of fabric for backing

27" x 31" piece of batting

To Add Interest

Select light fabrics in a variety of colors with stripes, checks, and plaids like those Uncle Frank might have chosen for his shirts. For a scrappier look, switch the positions of medium and dark fabrics in a few blocks, and rotate the direction of some blocks in your final quilt layout.

Cutting

All measurements include ¼"-wide seam allowances.

From *each* of the 4" x 7" light-print scraps, cut:
2 squares, 3" x 3"; cut in half diagonally to yield 4 triangles (48 total)

From *each* of the 4" x 4" medium-print scraps, cut:
4 squares, 1¼" x 1¼" (48 total)

From *each* of the 4" x 4" dark scraps, cut:
4 squares, 1¼" x 1¼" (48 total)

From *each* of the 3" x 5" medium or dark scraps, cut:
2 squares, 2" x 2" (24 total)

From the red print, cut:
2 strips, 1" x 42"; cut in half crosswise to yield 4 strips

From the green print, cut:
4 strips, 3½" x 42"
3 strips, 2" x 42"

Making the Blocks

Each block contains four different fabrics. Instructions are for making one block.

1. Sew two matching medium and two matching dark 1¼" squares together to make a four-patch unit measuring 2" square and press the seam allowances open. Make two matching four-patch units.

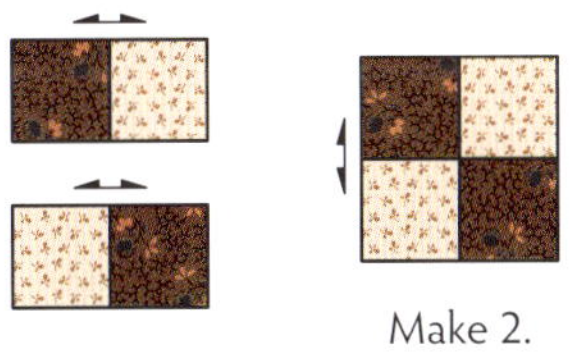

Make 2.

2. Sew the four-patch units from step 1 and two contrasting medium or dark 2" squares together to make a unit measuring 3½" square. Press the seam allowances open.

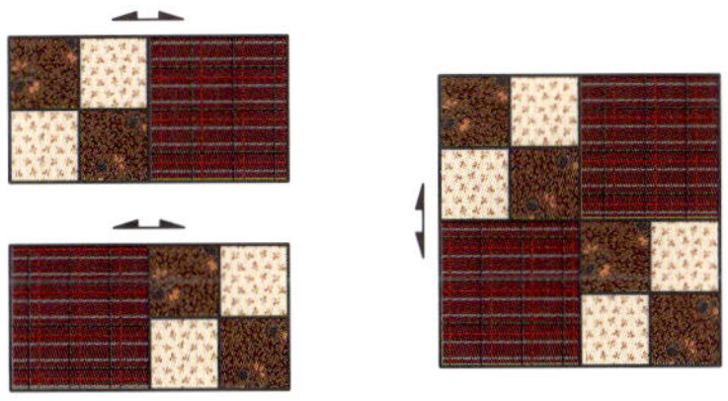

Make 12.

"Uncle Frank's Socks," pieced and quilted by Carol Hopkins

Finished quilt size: 20¼" x 24½"

Finished block size: 4¼" x 4¼"

3. Sew matching light 3" triangles to opposite sides of the unit. Press the seam allowances toward the light triangles.

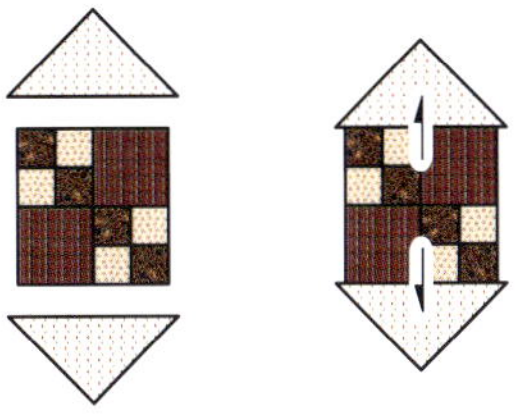

4. Sew matching light 3" triangles to the remaining two sides of the unit and press the seam allowances toward the triangles to make a block measuring 4¾" square. Make 12 blocks.

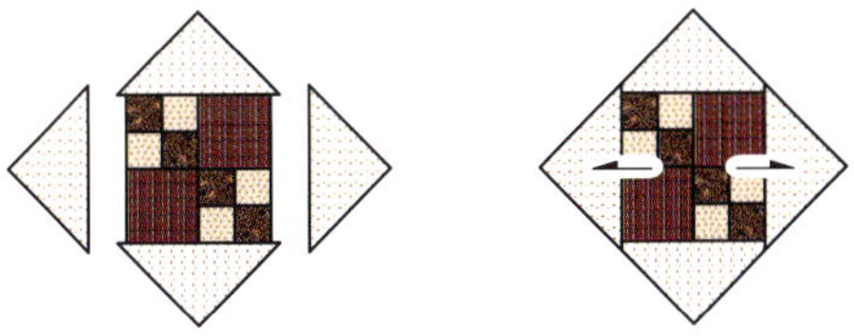

Make 12.

Assembling and Finishing the Quilt

For more help with any of the finishing steps, go to ShopMartingale.com/HowtoQuilt.

1. Arrange the blocks into four rows of three blocks, alternating the position of the four-patch units as shown. Sew the blocks together in rows and press the seam allowances open. Sew the rows together, pressing the seam allowances open after adding each row.

Quilt assembly

2. For the inner border, measure the length of the quilt top through the center and trim two of the red strips to this measurement. Sew the strips to the sides of the quilt and press the seam allowances toward the border.
3. Measure the width of the quilt through the center, including the just-added border pieces, and trim the two remaining red strips to this measurement. Sew the strips to the top and bottom of the quilt and press the seam allowances toward the border.
4. For the outer border, repeat steps 2 and 3 with the green 3½"-wide strips.

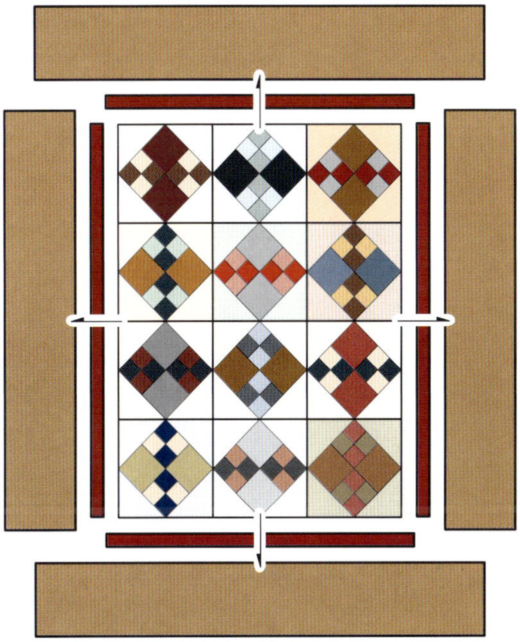

Adding borders

5. Layer the quilt top, batting, and backing. Baste the layers together and hand or machine quilt as desired. Trim the excess batting and backing fabric.
6. Use the green 2"-wide strips to bind the quilt. Add a hanging sleeve, if desired, and a label.

Susan's Courage

This quilt is named for my dear friend, Susan, who lost her battle with cancer. Susan's grace and courage as she fought her disease were amazing. She remains in the hearts of all who knew her.

Materials

Yardage is based on 42"-wide fabric.

1 yard of floral stripe *OR* ½ yard of nondirectional floral print for border

½ yard of dark-purple print for setting blocks

⅓ yard of light print for blocks

12 assorted dark scraps, at least 5" x 5" each, for blocks

12 assorted medium scraps, at least 4" x 4" each, for blocks

⅓ yard of light-purple print for binding

1 yard of fabric for backing

31" x 36" piece of batting

To Add Interest

Using a dark print for the setting squares and triangles will really make the blocks and light-colored border stand out.

Cutting

All measurements include ¼"-wide seam allowances.

From the light print, cut:

3 strips, 1⅞" x 42"; crosscut into 48 squares, 1⅞" x 1⅞". Cut each square in half diagonally to yield 96 triangles.

2 strips, 1½" x 42"; crosscut into 48 squares, 1½" x 1½"

From *each* of the dark scraps, cut:

4 squares, 1⅞" x 1⅞"; cut in half diagonally to yield 8 triangles (96 total)

From *each* of the medium scraps, cut:

4 squares, 1½" x 1½" (48 total)

From the dark-purple print, cut:

1 strip, 7" x 42"; crosscut into:

- 3 squares, 7" x 7"; cut into quarters diagonally to yield 12 triangles (2 are extra)
- 2 squares, 3¾" x 3¾"; cut in half diagonally to yield 4 triangles

1 strip, 4½" x 42"; crosscut into 6 squares, 4½" x 4½"

From the *lengthwise grain* of the floral stripe, cut*:

4 strips, 3" x 36"

From the light-purple print, cut:

4 strips, 2" x 42"

**If you're using a nondirectional print, cut the strips across the fabric width.*

Making the Blocks

One dark and one medium print are used in each block. Instructions are for making one block.

1. Sew a dark 1⅞" triangle to a light 1⅞" triangle to make a half-square-triangle unit. Press the seam allowances toward the dark triangle. Make eight matching units measuring 1½" square.

Make 8.

"Susan's Courage," pieced and quilted by Carol Hopkins

Finished quilt size: 22½" x 28⅛"

Finished block size: 4" x 4"

2. Arrange the half-square-triangle units, four medium 1½" squares, and four light 1½" squares as shown. Sew the pieces into rows and press the seam allowances open. Sew the rows together, pressing the seam allowances open, to make a block measuring 4½" square. Make 12 blocks.

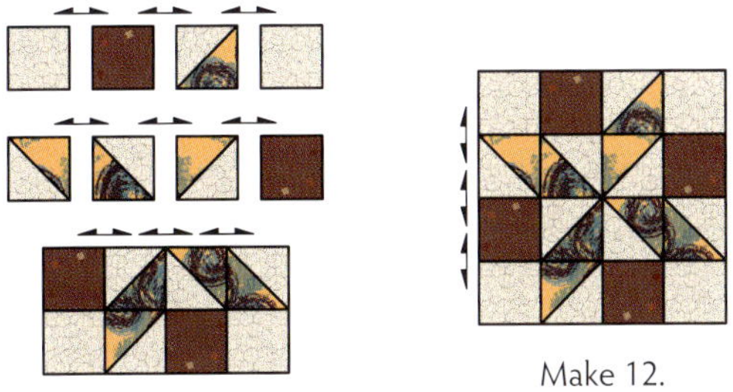

Make 12.

Assembling and Finishing the Quilt

For more help with any of the finishing steps, go to ShopMartingale.com/HowtoQuilt.

1. Arrange the blocks and dark-purple 4½" squares in diagonal rows as shown below. Add the purple 7" side triangles and 3¾" corner triangles.
2. Sew the blocks, setting squares, and side triangles together in diagonal rows. Press the seam allowances open.
3. Sew the rows together, pressing the seam allowances open after adding each row. Add the corner triangles and press the seam allowances toward the triangles.

Quilt assembly

4. Trim the quilt top if necessary, leaving a ¼" seam allowance beyond the points of the blocks.
5. Measure the length of the quilt top through the center and trim two of the floral strips to this measurement. Sew the strips to the sides of the quilt and press the seam allowances toward the border.
6. Measure the width of the quilt top through the center, including the just-added border pieces, and trim the two remaining floral strips to this measurement. Sew the strips to the top and bottom of the quilt and press the seam allowances toward the border.

Adding borders

7. Layer the quilt top, batting, and backing. Baste the layers together and hand or machine quilt as desired. Trim the excess batting and backing fabric.
8. Use the light-purple 2"-wide strips to bind the quilt. Add a hanging sleeve, if desired, and a label.

Caissons Rolling

Caissons were two-wheeled carts used to carry heavy ammunition chests, spare wheels, pick axes, shovels, tar buckets, and other miscellaneous tools needed to repair the roads that soldiers traveled on. This equipment weighed so much that six horses were needed to pull the load carried in a single caisson.

Materials

Yardage is based on 42"-wide fabric.

1⅛ yards of red-and-brown stripe *OR* ⅝ yard of nondirectional red-and-brown print for border

⅝ yard of light print for blocks

⅓ yard of gold print for setting squares

5 assorted red, blue, or brown strips, at least 3" x 21" each, for blocks

5 assorted red, blue, or brown scraps, at least 7" x 7" each, for blocks

⅓ yard of brown print for binding

1⅛ yards of fabric for backing

40" x 40" piece of batting

To Add Interest

Select a busy floral or vine print for the background to disguise the numerous seam lines in the pieced block.

Cutting

All measurements include ¼"-wide seam allowances.

From the light print, cut:

2 strips, 2½" x 42"; crosscut into 20 squares, 2½" x 2½"

9 strips, 1½" x 42"; crosscut into:

- 20 rectangles, 1½" x 2½"
- 180 squares, 1½" x 1½"

From *each* of the red, blue, or brown strips, cut:

8 squares, 2½" x 2½" (40 total)

From *each* of the 7" x 7" red, blue, or brown scraps, cut:

1 square, 2½" x 2½" (5 total)

8 squares, 1½" x 1½" (40 total)

From the gold print, cut:

4 squares, 8½" x 8½"

From the red-and-brown stripe, cut *on the lengthwise grain:**

4 strips, 4¼" x 41"

From the brown print, cut:

4 strips, 2" x 42"

**If you're using a nondirectional print, cut the strips across the fabric width.*

Making the Blocks

The light print is paired with two contrasting red, blue, or brown prints in each block. Instructions are for making one block.

1. Make a flying-geese unit with two matching dark 1½" squares (cut from the 7" x 7" scraps) and one light 1½" x 2½" rectangle as shown. Make four matching flying-geese units.

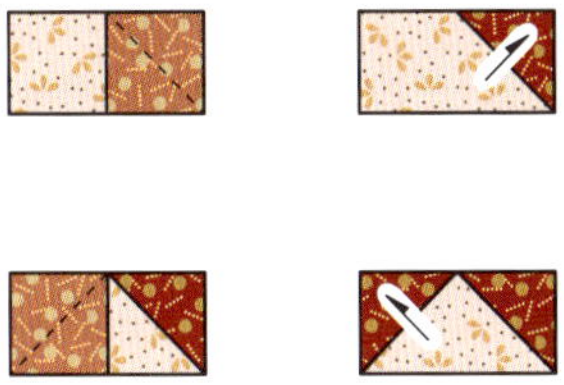

Make 4.

2. Arrange the four units from step 1, a matching dark 2½" square, and four 1½" light squares as shown on page 65. Sew the pieces together into rows, and press the seam allowances open. Sew

"Caissons Rolling," pieced by Carol Hopkins and quilted by Lisa Ramsey

Finished quilt size: 32" x 32"

Finished block size: 8" x 8"

the rows together, pressing the seam allowances open, to make a unit measuring 4½" square.

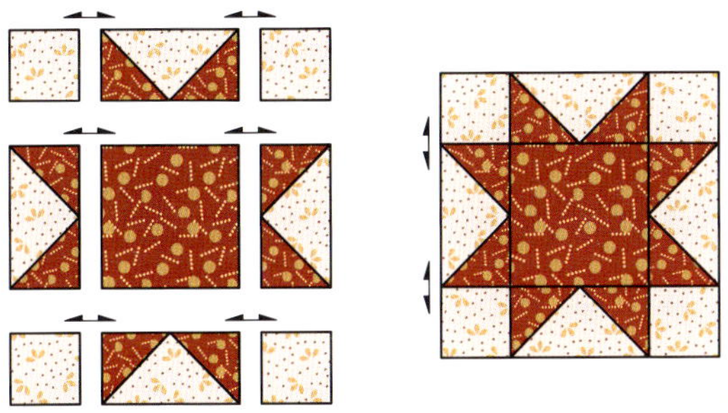

3. Sew a 1½" light square to each corner of a contrasting 2½" dark square (cut from the 3" x 21" strips) to make a Square-in-a-Square unit. Press as shown after adding each square. Make eight units.

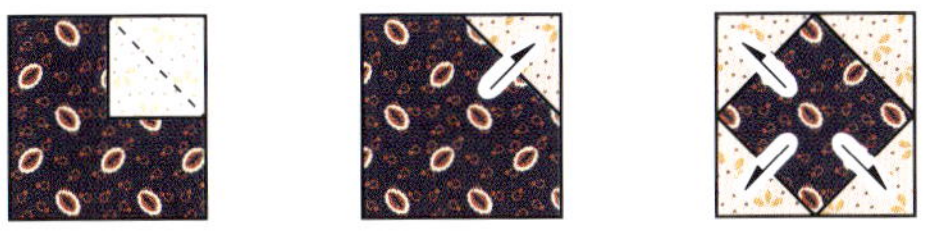

Make 8.

4. Sew the Square-in-a-Square units together into four pairs of two units each. Press the seam allowances open.

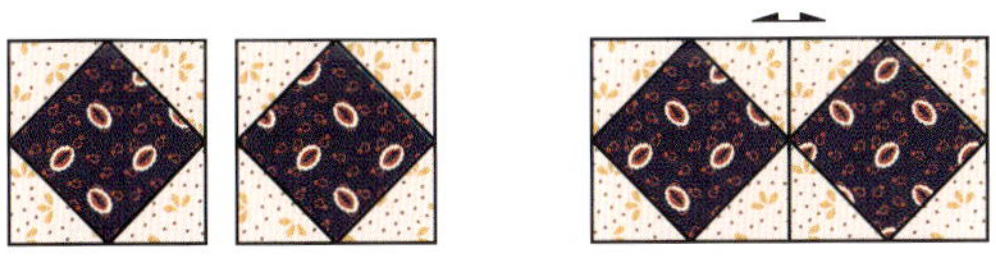

Make 4.

5. Arrange the units from steps 2 and 4 and four light 2½" squares as shown. Sew the pieces together into rows, and press the seam allowances open. Sew the rows together, pressing the seam allowances open to make a block measuring 8½" square. Make five blocks.

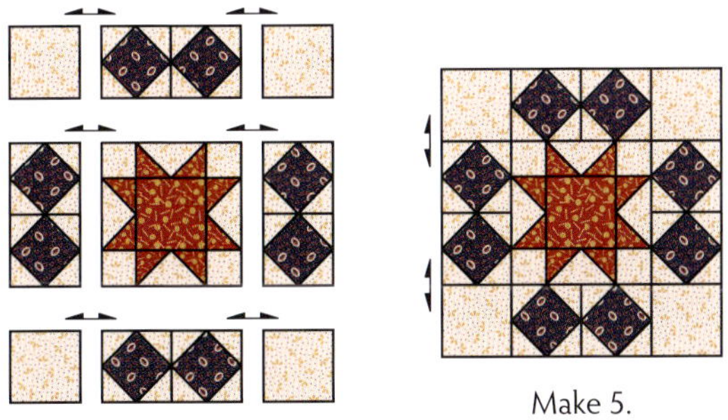

Make 5.

Assembling and Finishing the Quilt

For more help with any of the finishing steps, go to ShopMartingale.com/HowtoQuilt.

1. Arrange the blocks and gold 8½" squares in rows. Sew the blocks in each row together and press the seam allowances open. Sew the rows together, pressing the seam allowances open after adding each row.
2. For the border, measure the length of the quilt top through the center and add 9". Trim two red-and-brown strips to this measurement. Sew the strips to the sides of the quilt, right sides together, matching the centers and starting and stopping ¼" from the corners of the quilt.
3. Measure the quilt width, without the border, and add 9". Trim the two remaining red-and-brown strips to this measurement. Center and pin these strips to the top and bottom of the quilt, right sides together. Sew these strips to the quilt, starting and stopping ¼" from the corners of the quilt, and press the seam allowances toward the border.
4. Miter the border at each corner of the quilt.

5. Layer the quilt top, batting, and backing. Baste the layers together and hand or machine quilt as desired. Trim the excess batting and backing fabric.
6. Use the brown 2"-wide strips to bind the quilt. Add a hanging sleeve, if desired, and a label.

Rosie Finch

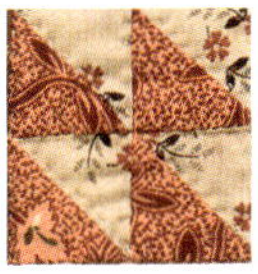

My husband and I sat at the window of a gift shop on the top of Sandia Crest in the mountains of Albuquerque, New Mexico, watching for rosy finches to gather at the nearby bird feeders. As I worked on this quilt back in our hotel room, it reminded me of the soft colors of those small birds.

Materials

Yardage is based on 42"-wide fabric.

⅓ yard of tan print for outer border

¼ yard of brown print for inner border and binding

18 assorted light scraps, at least 6" x 6" each, for blocks

18 assorted medium or dark scraps, at least 6" x 6" each, for blocks

⅞ yard of fabric for backing

25" x 29" piece of batting

To Add Interest

Break away from calm, neutral backgrounds, and don't be afraid to use bold prints in these small triangles. Challenge yourself to make the blocks for this quilt from your scrap bag!

Cutting

All measurements include ¼"-wide seam allowances.

From *17* of the light scraps, cut:

1 square, 2⅞" x 2⅞"; cut in half diagonally to yield 2 triangles (34 total; 17 are extra)

From *each* of the 18 light scraps, cut:

2 squares, 1⅞" x 1⅞"; cut in half diagonally to yield 4 triangles (72 total)

From *17* of the medium or dark scraps, cut:

1 square, 2⅞" x 2⅞"; cut in half diagonally to yield 2 triangles (34 total; 17 are extra)

From *each* of the 18 medium or dark scraps, cut:

2 squares, 1⅞" x 1⅞"; cut in half diagonally to yield 4 triangles (72 total)

From the brown print, cut:

2 strips, 1" x 42"; cut in half crosswise to yield 4 strips

2 strips, 2" x 42"

From the tan print, cut:

3 strips, 3" x 42"; cut *1* strip in half crosswise to yield 2 strips, 3" x 21"

Making the Blocks

1. Sew a light 2⅞" triangle to a medium or dark 2⅞" triangle to make a half-square-triangle unit. Press the seam allowances toward the dark triangle. Make 17 half-square-triangle units measuring 2½" square.

Make 17.

2. Sew a light 1⅞" triangle to a medium or dark 1⅞" triangle to make a half-square-triangle unit. Press the seam allowances toward the dark triangle. Make four matching half-square-triangle units measuring 1½" square.

Make 4.

"Rosie Finch," pieced and quilted by Carol Hopkins

Finished quilt size: 16½" x 20½"

Finished block size: 2" x 2"

3. Arrange the half-square-triangle units from step 2 as shown and sew them together into rows, pressing the seam allowances open. Sew the rows together and press the seam allowances open to make a block measuring 2½" square. Make 18 blocks.

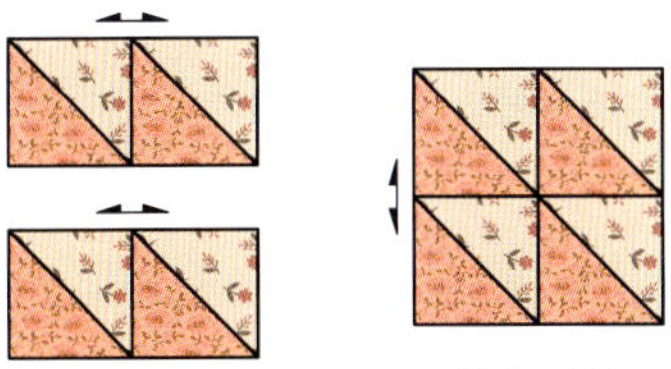

Make 18.

Assembling and Finishing the Quilt

For more help with any of the finishing steps, go to ShopMartingale.com/HowtoQuilt.

1. Arrange the blocks as shown. Sew the blocks together in rows and press the seam allowances open. Sew the rows together, pressing the seam allowances open after adding each row.

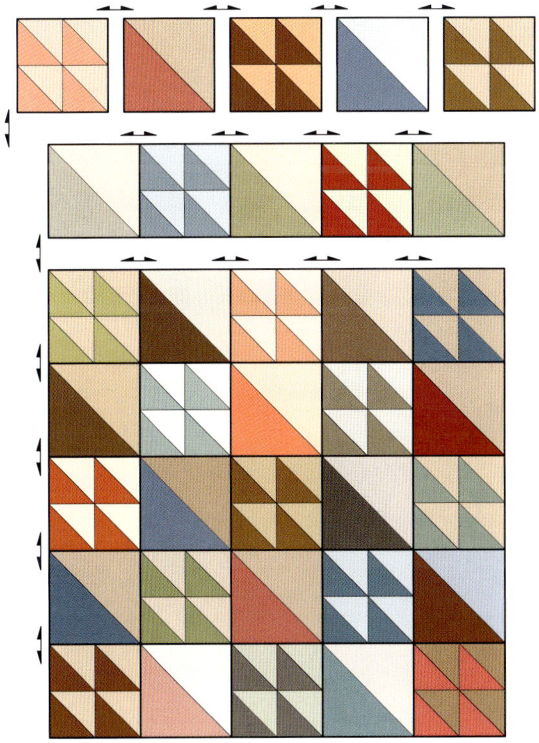

Quilt assembly

2. For the inner border, measure the length of the quilt top through the center and trim two of the brown 1"-wide strips to this measurement. Sew the strips to the sides of the quilt and press the seam allowances toward the border.
3. Measure the width of the quilt through the center, including the just-added border pieces, and trim the two remaining brown 1"-wide strips to this measurement. Sew the strips to the top and bottom of the quilt and press the seam allowances toward the border.
4. For the outer border, repeat steps 2 and 3 using the tan 3"-wide strips.

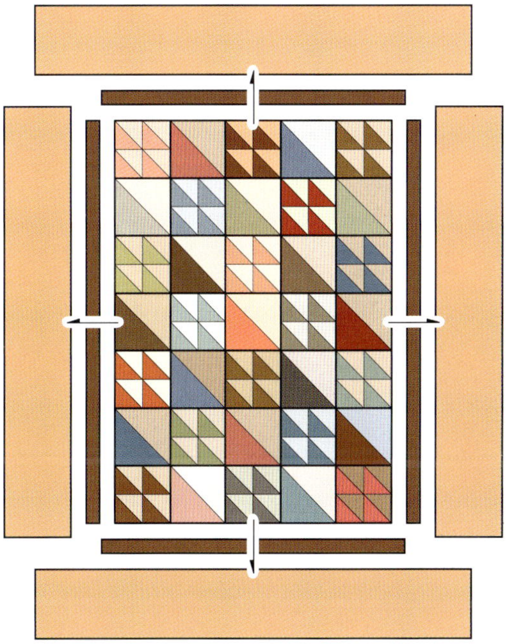

Adding borders

5. Layer the quilt top, batting, and backing. Baste the layers together and hand or machine quilt as desired. Trim the excess batting and backing fabric.
6. Use the brown 2"-wide strips to bind the quilt. Add a hanging sleeve, if desired, and a label.

Elizabeth's Baskets

One of the first quilt patterns I designed, "Baskets for Betsy," was named for my youngest sister. This pattern, based on an unusual basket block seen in an antique quilt, is also named for Betsy using her "grown-up" name.

Materials

Yardage is based on 42"-wide fabric.

1⅜ yards of green directional print *OR* ¾ yard of green nondirectional print for outer border and binding

⅝ yard of small-scale green print for setting squares and triangles

½ yard of light print for blocks

⅓ yard of black print for inner border

20 assorted medium scraps, at least 3" x 7" each, for blocks

20 assorted dark scraps, at least 6" x 8" each, for blocks

1¼ yards of fabric for backing

39" x 45" piece of batting

To Add Interest

Using large prints for some of the basket bases will break up the uniformity of the blocks and create movement in the quilt.

Cutting

All measurements include ¼"-wide seam allowances.

From the light print, cut:

4 strips, 1½" x 42"; crosscut into:

- 40 rectangles, 1½" x 2½"
- 20 squares, 1½" x 1½"

3 strips, 1⅞" x 42"; crosscut into 50 squares, 1⅞" x 1⅞". Cut each square in half diagonally to yield 100 triangles.

From *each* of the medium scraps, cut:

3 squares, 1⅞" x 1⅞"; cut in half diagonally to yield 6 triangles (120 total)

From *each* of the dark scraps, cut:

1 square, 2⅞" x 2⅞"; cut in half diagonally to yield 2 triangles (use one of each print for 40 total; 20 are extra)

3 squares, 1½" x 1½" (60 total)

1 square, 1⅞" x 1⅞"; cut in half diagonally to yield 2 triangles (use one of each print for 40 total; 20 are extra)

From the small-scale green print, cut:

1 strip, 7" x 42"; crosscut into:

- 4 squares, 7" x 7"; cut into quarters diagonally to yield 16 triangles (2 are extra)
- 2 squares, 3¾" x 3¾"; cut in half diagonally to yield 4 triangles

2 strips 4½" x 42"; crosscut into 12 squares, 4½" x 4½"

From the black print, cut:

4 strips, 1¼" x 42"

From the green directional print, cut*:

4 strips, 3½" x 42"

4 strips, 2" x 42"

**The sample quilt uses a directional print, so the side border strips were cut on the lengthwise grain and the top and bottom strips were cut crosswise. This allows the motif to be positioned right side up all around the quilt. You'll need 1⅜ yards of fabric to cut directional-print border strips. Cut 2 strips, 3½" x 42", on the crosswise grain. From the remaining fabric, cut 2 strips, 3½" x 38", on the lengthwise grain. Also, cut 4 strips, 2" x 38", for binding.*

"Elizabeth's Baskets," pieced by Carol Hopkins and quilted by Lisa Ramsey

Finished quilt size: 30⅝" x 36¼"

Finished block size: 4" x 4"

Making the Basket Blocks

The light print is paired with a different dark and medium print in each of the blocks. Instructions are for making one block.

1. Sew a dark 1⅞" triangle to a light 1⅞" triangle to make a half-square-triangle unit measuring 1½" square. Press the seam allowances toward the dark triangle.

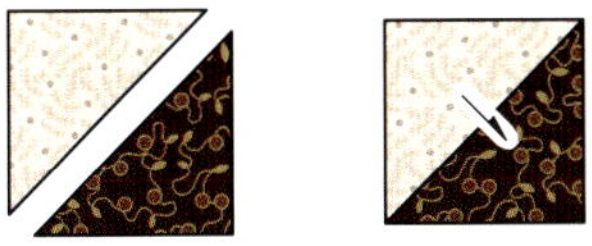

Make 1.

2. Sew a medium 1⅞" triangle to a light 1⅞" triangle to make a half-square-triangle unit. Press the seam allowances toward the medium triangle. Make four matching units measuring 1½" square.

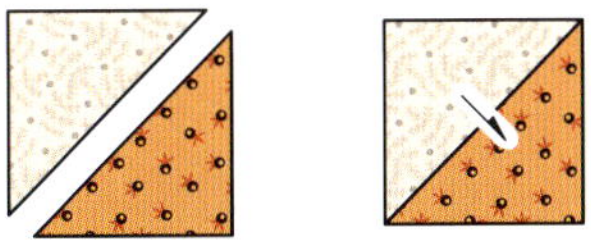

Make 4.

3. Sew the half-square-triangles from step 2 into pairs as shown. Press the seam allowances open.

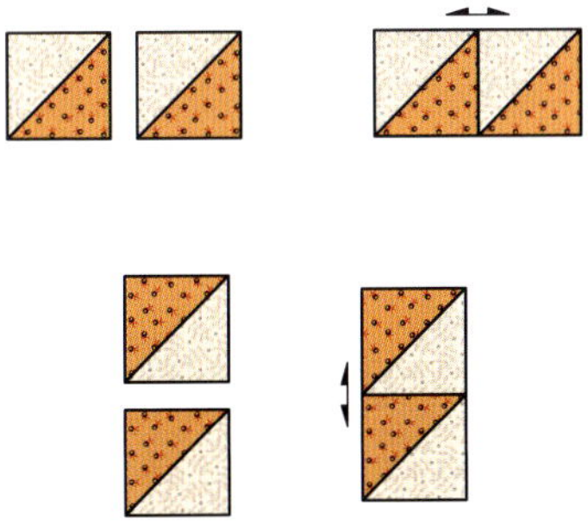

4. Sew two medium 1⅞" triangles to a dark 1½" square. Press the seam allowances open. Trim off the dog-ear points.

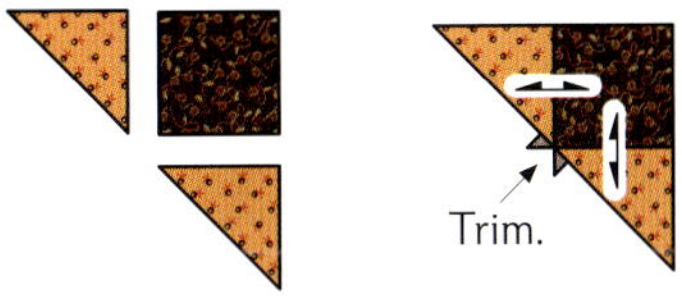

5. Sew the unit from step 4 to a matching dark 2⅞" triangle. Press the seam allowances toward the large triangle. Trim off the dog-ear points.

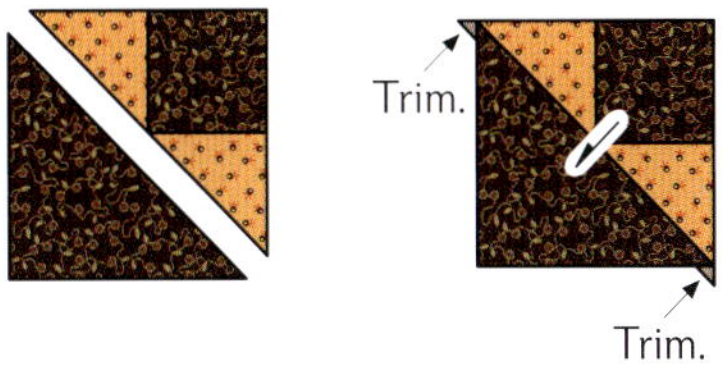

6. Arrange two light 1½" x 2½" rectangles and one light 1½" square; the units from steps 3 and 5; and two matching dark 1½" squares as shown. Sew the pieces together into rows and press the seam allowances open. Sew the rows together, pressing the seam allowances open, to make a block measuring 4½" square. Make 20 blocks.

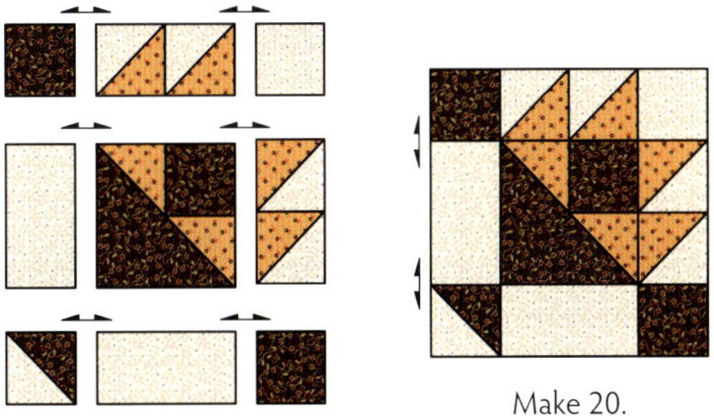

Make 20.

Assembling and Finishing the Quilt

For more help with any of the finishing steps, go to ShopMartingale.com/HowtoQuilt.

1. Arrange the blocks and green 4½" squares in diagonal rows as shown on page 74. Add the green 7" side triangles and 3¾" corner triangles.
2. Sew the blocks, setting squares, and side triangles together in diagonal rows. Press the seam allowances open.

3. Sew the rows together, pressing the seam allowances open after adding each row. Add the green 3¾" corner triangles and press the seam allowances toward the triangles.

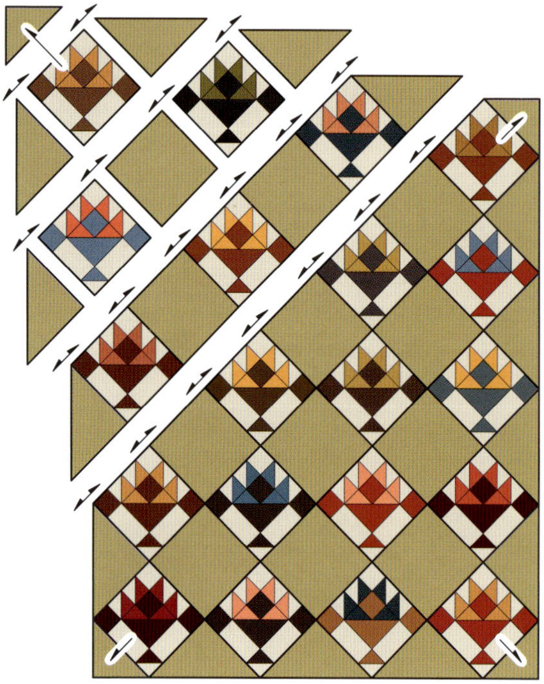

Quilt assembly

4. Trim the quilt top if necessary, leaving a ¼" seam allowance beyond the points of the blocks.

5. For the inner border, measure the length of the quilt top through the center and trim two black strips to this measurement. Sew the strips to the sides of the quilt and press the seam allowances toward the border.

6. Measure the width of the quilt top through the center, including the just-added border pieces, and trim the two remaining black strips to this measurement. Sew the strips to the top and bottom of the quilt and press the seam allowances toward the border.

7. For the outer border, measure the length of the quilt top through the center and trim the two 3½"-wide strips cut *lengthwise* from the green directional print to this measurement. Sew the strips to the sides of the quilt and press the seam allowances toward the outer border.

8. Measure the width of the quilt top through the center, including the just-added border pieces, and trim the two 3½"-wide strips cut *crosswise* from the green directional print to this measurement. Sew the strips to the top and bottom of the quilt and press the seam allowances toward the outer border.

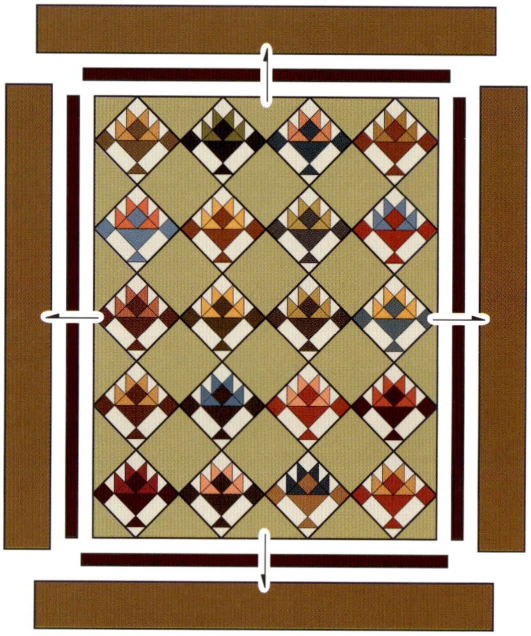

Adding borders

9. Layer the quilt top, batting, and backing. Baste the layers together and hand or machine quilt as desired. Trim the excess batting and backing fabric.

10. Use the green 2"-wide strips to bind the quilt. Add a hanging sleeve, if desired, and a label.

Melissa's Locket

My beautiful niece Melissa loves lockets. Her first one came packaged with a children's book about a little girl with a locket, and at age three, she wore the locket while she pretended to read the book. She might have gotten her love of lockets from her mother, who wears a locket containing a picture of her three daughters. That locket is indented by little bite marks from Melissa's teething days.

Materials

Yardage is based on 42"-wide fabric.

1⅞ yards of brown stripe *OR* 1½ yards of nondirectional print for border

1⅛ yards of light print for block backgrounds

32 assorted dark scraps, at least 8" x 8" each, for blocks

32 assorted red scraps, at least 5" x 5" each, for blocks

32 assorted light scraps, at least 5" x 5" each, for blocks

½ yard of dark-brown print for binding

2⅞ yards of fabric for backing

52" x 65" piece of batting

To Add Interest

When selecting fabrics for the blocks, include multicolored, large-scale dark prints; use red prints that range from pink to dark red.

Cutting

All measurements include ¼"-wide seam allowances.

From the light background print, cut:

1 strip, 9¾" x 42"; crosscut into 4 squares, 9¾" x 9¾". Cut each square into quarters diagonally to yield 16 triangles (2 are extra).

1 strip, 5⅛" x 42"; crosscut into 2 squares, 5⅛" x 5⅛". Cut each square in half diagonally to yield 4 triangles.

4 strips, 3⅞" x 42"; crosscut into 32 squares, 3⅞" x 3⅞". Cut each square in half diagonally to yield 64 triangles.

2 strips, 2½" x 42"

From *each* of the dark scraps, cut:

1 square, 3⅞" x 3⅞"; cut in half diagonally to yield 2 triangles (64 total)

2 rectangles, 1½" x 3½" (64 total)

2 rectangles, 1½" x 2½" (64 total)

From *each* of the red scraps, cut:

4 squares, 1⅞" x 1⅞"; cut in half diagonally to yield 8 triangles (256 total)

From *each* of the light scraps, cut:

4 squares, 1⅞" x 1⅞"; cut in half diagonally to yield 8 triangles (256 total)

From the *lengthwise grain* of the brown stripe, cut:

4 strips, 5" x 64", for mitered borders *OR* 4 strips, 5" x 52", for nonmitered borders

From the dark-brown print, cut:

6 strips, 2" x 42"

Making the Blocks

Each block contains different light and red prints for the pinwheels framed by a dark print. The same background fabric is used for the large triangle corners of each block. Directions are for making one block.

1. Sew a red 1⅞" triangle to a light 1⅞" triangle to make a half-square-triangle unit. Press the seam allowances toward the red triangle. Make eight matching units measuring 1½" square.

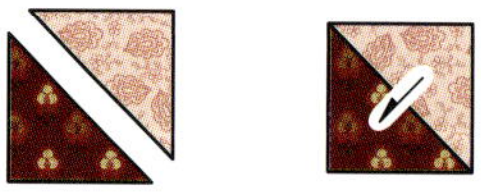

Make 8.

"Melissa's Locket," pieced by Carol Hopkins and quilted by Lisa Ramsey

Finished quilt size: 43½" x 57"

Finished block size: 6" x 6"

2. Arrange four of the half-square-triangle units as shown. Sew the units together in rows, pressing the seam allowances open. Sew the rows together to make a pinwheel measuring 2½" square. Press the seam allowances open. Make two matching pinwheels for each block.

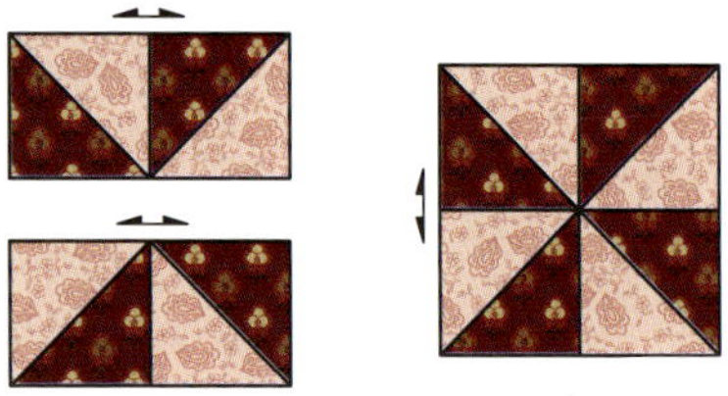

Make 2.

3. Sew a dark 1½" x 2½" rectangle to the right side of each pinwheel from step 2. Press the seam allowances open.

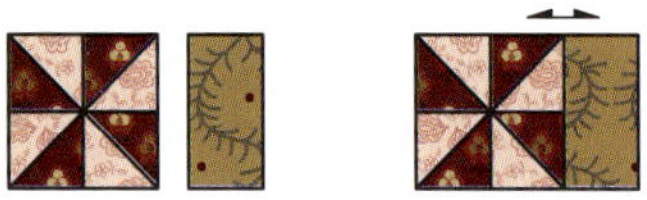

Make 2.

4. Sew a matching dark 1½" x 3½" rectangle to the top of each step 3 unit and press the seam allowances open.

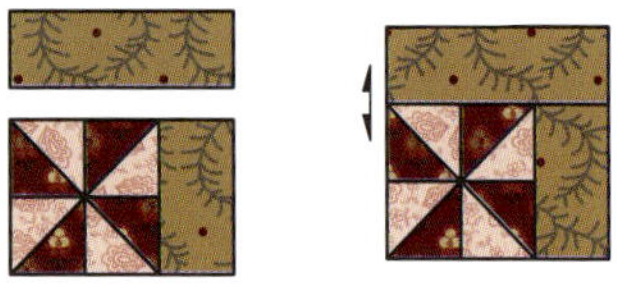

Make 2.

5. Sew a dark triangle to a background 3⅞" triangle to make a half-square-triangle unit. Press the seam allowances toward the dark triangle. Make two matching units measuring 3½" square.

6. Arrange the units from step 4 and half-square-triangle units from step 5 as shown. Sew the pieces together into rows and press the seam allowances open. Sew the rows together and press the seam allowances open to make a block measuring 6½" square. Make 32 blocks.

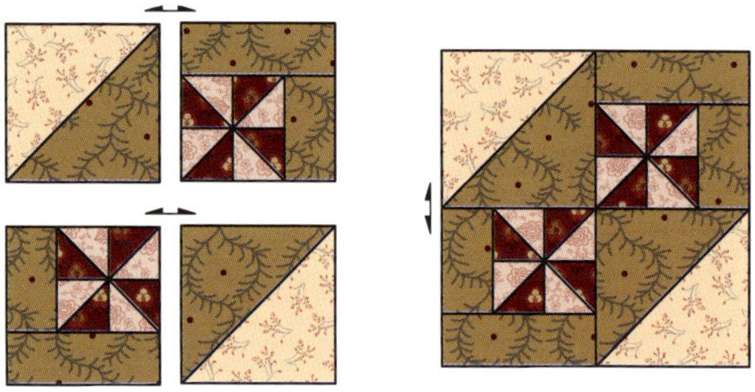

Make 32.

Assembling and Finishing the Quilt

For more help with any of the finishing steps, go to ShopMartingale.com/HowtoQuilt.

1. Arrange the blocks in diagonal rows as shown below. Add the background 9¾" side triangles and 5⅛" corner triangles.
2. Sew the blocks and side triangles together in diagonal rows. Press the seam allowances open.
3. Sew the rows together, pressing the seam allowances open after adding each row. Add the corner triangles and press the seam allowances toward the triangles.

Quilt assembly

4. Trim the quilt top if necessary, leaving a ¼" seam allowance beyond the points of the blocks.

5. Measure the width of the quilt top through the center and trim the two background 2½"-wide strips to this measurement. Sew these strips to the top and bottom of the quilt, starting and stopping ¼" from the corners of the quilt, and press the seam allowances toward the border.

6. Measure the length of the quilt top through the center and add 11". Trim two brown 5"-wide strips to this measurement. Sew the strips to the sides of the quilt, right sides together, matching the centers and starting and stopping ¼" from the corners of the quilt.

7. Measure the quilt width, without the border, and add 11". Trim the two remaining brown strips to this measurement. Center and pin these strips to the top and bottom of the quilt, right sides together. Sew these strips to the quilt, starting and stopping ¼" from the corners of the quilt, and press the seam allowances toward the border.

8. Miter the borders at each corner of the quilt.

Adding borders

9. Layer the quilt top, batting, and backing. Baste the layers together and hand or machine quilt as desired. Trim the excess batting and backing fabric.

10. Use the dark-brown 2"-wide strips to bind the quilt. Add a hanging sleeve, if desired, and a label.

Optional Butted-Corner Border

If you've chosen a nondirectional border print, you may prefer not to miter the quilt border. Follow these instructions instead.

1. Measure the length of the quilt top through the center and trim two border strips to this measurement. Sew the strips to the sides of the quilt and press the seam allowances toward the border.

2. Measure the width of the quilt top through the center, including the just-added border pieces, and trim the two remaining border strips to this measurement. Sew the strips to the top and bottom of the quilt and press the seam allowances toward the border.

About the Author

Carol Hopkins lives with her husband, Edward, in West Lafayette, Indiana, where she is a professor of Literacy and Language Education at Purdue University. She enjoys spending her spare time with her three adult children and grandchildren, and pursuing her 36-year love of quiltmaking.

She has published two best-selling books, *Civil War Legacies* (2012) and *Civil War Legacies II* (2014), with Martingale, and more than 95 patterns for small and large quilts marketed as "Civil War Legacies" and "Vintage Legacies" for her company, Carol Hopkins Designs. She is known for her scrappy, pieced-quilt designs, each of which includes dozens of eighteenth- or nineteenth-century reproduction fabrics. Carol's quilts and patterns have appeared worldwide in publications including *Australian Quilters Companion, Quilter's Newsletter Magazine, Quiltmaker, Quiltmaker's 100 Blocks, Miniature Quilts,* and *The Quilter.*

To learn more about Carol and see more of her work, visit www.carolhopkinsdesigns.com.

Acknowledgments

I am so appreciative of the opportunity that the amazing Martingale staff has provided me to share this third collection of quilt patterns. In addition to providing incredible technical support, they are the nicest, most encouraging, friendliest, and fun-loving people anyone could ever hope to work with. Working with them again on this book is like attending a quilt family reunion.

And, speaking of families, I thank mine for their gifts of love, support and encouragement. They've learned to say magic words like, "That quilt looks so old," and "No, we don't mind giving up half of the kitchen table for the computer, piles of manuscript pages, and eraser (rather than food) crumbs."

I am so fortunate to have Lisa Ramsey, a super-talented machine quilter, add her original designs to my quilts. I thank her for her friendship, her wonderful feather designs, and her willingness to be on call when deadlines near.

Special thanks to Pati Violick (Marcus Fabrics), Jo Morton (Andover Fabrics), Laura Jaquinto (Windham Fabrics), and Edyta Sitar (Moda Fabrics) for your generosity in sending me your newest reproduction fabrics. You have no idea how many hours I spend oohing and aahing over them, and rearranging fat quarters again and again into wonderful combinations before I actually cut into them!

To my quilting friends, I thank you for the fun times we have traveling to quilt shops and shows, daydreaming about quilts we want to make, exchanging blocks, and sharing life's ups and downs.

And last, but never least, I thank my parents, Anne and Bill Horgan, for buying me my first sewing machine and always being there for me. I miss you every day.